WHEN SATAN
TRIES TO SILENCE YOU

WHEN SATAN
TRIES TO SILENCE YOU

TONY E. LUCAS

XULON PRESS

Xulon Press
2301 Lucien Way #415
Maitland, FL 32751
407.339.4217
www.xulonpress.com

Paperback ISBN-13: 978-1-66285-309-8
Ebook ISBN-13: 978-1-66285-310-4

Introduction

A Desert Place

I think it's safe to say that everyone has experienced times in their life when they felt all alone. We've all walked in those dry, barren places and felt as if we are the only person in the world who has ever been there. Our desires change, our vision is blurred, we hunger and thirst, but satisfaction is hard to come by. Nothing makes us happy, we can't see past the nose on our face, and yes, we hunger and thirst, but we're just not sure what it is that would make us full, hydrated, and totally satisfied. How can it be? We always lived life to the fullest and enjoyed being around people. A good conversation, laughing with our friends and family, visiting with our neighbors; all these things seem to be in the distant past. Serving God, reaching out to others with the gospel, just trying to do our part to make a positive impact in the world around us had a common place in our hearts and life, but something has changed. Avoiding any contact with people in general tends to be the path of choice, and soon we consider that path to be the total norm for our lives.

I've come to the conclusion that Satan is doing everything he can to silence all of us. If he can keep us walking around in the wilderness and feeling as if we no longer have anything positive to say, friends, that is exactly what he will do. Satan is out to steal, kill, and destroy! He will rob us of our joy and cause us to start believing we are useless. It is my desire to share some things about my life with you in the pages ahead that will cause you to see the truth about yourself. Hopefully you will see you are not alone on this journey. We all have our own set of issues. It's easy to get turned around in the desert, and if we're not careful, we will end up wandering around there for years. With each passing day we are getting older, our opportunities to make a positive impact are swiftly passing, and Satan is perfectly satisfied. Has he been successful in silencing you? If so, I hope my story will challenge you to change your way of thinking. Let go and let God take control. Open up your hearts and minds to the

truth that God wants to set you free. I challenge you to be a blessing today and the rest of your life. Let's get out of the desert and move on up to higher ground!

—Tony

Chapter 1

The Beginning

Everything has a beginning. Our life began because God saw fit to create us. I've never been able to understand how anyone could not believe in creation. We see it in everything. In the springtime, we see new life springing forth from the ground as the flowers begin to pop through the surface of the soil and begin to bloom. The trees show signs of new life with each bud that develops on every limb, and those buds eventually turn into new leaves. The grass that has been dormant all winter long begins to grow again, and the process of life and creation continues exactly the way God designed it to be.

It was not until I was standing in the delivery room with my wife as she was giving birth to our first son Zachary that I fully understood how awesome God really is. I watched as she suffered and endured the pain that childbirth brings on. While I didn't feel the pain, I could tell what Lynette was going through was the real deal. Doing everything I could to bring some sort of comfort to her, as hard as I tried, I realized that it was out of my control. As time went by, the contractions started coming faster and lasted longer, making things get worse and worse. Overwhelmed by what was taking place, I finally understood that what I had read in the Bible about women being cursed with the pain of childbirth because of sin was a fact (Gen. 3:16). I'm sure it wasn't soon enough for Lynette, but we soon heard the doctor say, "I can see the head," and before we knew it, we heard Zachary cry for the first time.

For nine months prior to Zachary's birth, Lynette and I knew there was a new life forming inside of her. We would go to doctor's appointments and got to hear the heartbeat. Her ultrasound was scheduled, and we got to watch a gray-and-white blob on a screen and was told it was our baby. Again, we could hear the heartbeat, and while I could not tell anything about what I was seeing on the screen, I understood what that heartbeat meant. New life was being formed, God had allowed it to happen, and our son was growing day by day. However, when I heard his cry for the very first time and saw him squirming around in the doctor's hands, I understood it was a new beginning for us. Immediately, I became a dad for the first time. I witnessed a human coming into this world and heard that human's voice for the first time. Needless to say, the tears were flowing like a river down my face as I understood how real God was at that moment.

In the very first verse of the Bible, Genesis 1:1, we read about "The Beginning." This verse says, "In the beginning God created the heavens and the earth." On down in Genesis chapter 1, we see in verse 26 that for the very first time, God started talking about creating man. In verse 27 we read, "So God created man in his own image, in the image of God created he him; male and female created he them." But it is verse 28 that came to mind as I was standing there, listening to my son cry his little heart out. I realized for the first time that I was numbered with those who are spoken of in verse 28 of the very first book and chapter of the Bible. "God blessed them" (speaking of the male and female he had created in his own image). Not only did he bless them, but He said to them, "Be fruitful, and multiply, and replenish the earth." Suddenly I realized that God allowed me to be a part of the process of multiplying and replenishing the earth He had created, and what a blessing that has been for me.

I've always been thankful for the life God has given me. While this particular moment in time was not the beginning of my life, it was certainly the beginning of how I truly understood that everything is a blessing given to us by God. Satan would like to rob us of these types of events and keep us silent about the miracle moments we experience, but like the first cry that came from Zachary; we too need to let our voices be heard as we share the love of Christ with others.

Genesis 1:1—"In the beginning God created the heaven and the earth."

Think About What You Just Read

A Minute of Meditation

Pause for just a minute and think about a miracle moment you have experienced at some point in your life. Have you ever shared that moment with anyone? God gave you a blessing; it was a miracle that you witnessed with your own eyes. Why not share it with someone? Others may need to hear about your experience. It's a part of your testimony to the world around you. How did God use that miracle moment to get your attention about the truths that are recorded in the Bible? Satan is perfectly satisfied if you never share these moments with anyone. We need to understand that we have a voice that God has given us to offer praise to Him for what He continually does in and through our lives. Don't let Satan silence you! I want to challenge you to speak freely of the goodness of God and share your story with someone. It will be a blessing to you.

Chapter 2

Earlier in Time

July 19, 1963 was the first day of my life. It was the first time my mother and dad heard my cry but certainly not the last. Growing up here in the mountains of West Virginia offered a wonderful way of life for me. I have go back to sometime in 1966 for some of my earliest memories. My grandparents, Mom Maw and Pop Paw Counts, owned and operated a little local grocery store. My mother worked there at the store, and I asked her about these memories I had of going there with her in the mornings. Mom confirmed that I was three years old at the time, but I can remember her taking me to the back stock area of the store every morning and laying me down in a bed she made out of heavy, thick quilts. Pop Paw Counts would always let me put my hand in the candy jars and pull out a hand full of candy, pretty much every day. I didn't know it at the time, but being the baby of my family gave me some special privileges that my older sisters didn't have. Just little fringe benefits for being the youngest grandchild, I suppose, and the only grandson at that!

Other memories I have go back to was when I was four and five years old. From what I remember of my Granddaddy Lucas, he wasn't the happiest man in the world. I'd have to say he was pretty grumpy, actually. I'm not sure why, other than he was not in the best of health, and knowing how grouchy I am when I'm sick, I would say that contributed to his grumpy attitude.

However, I remember a time when Granddaddy held me on his lap while he cut the grass on his riding lawn mower. I think that may have something to do with the fact that I enjoy getting on my riding mower today and cutting my own grass.

Another special memory I have that was right about the same time was one of my Pop Paw Counts getting things ready to take me on a fishing trip. He had been packing things in the car and Mom Maw was packing a picnic basket for us to take on our fishing trip. We were all standing in their kitchen when we heard a knock on the front door. Pop Paw went to the door, and standing there was his sister and her son who just stopped by for a visit. Back in those days, a visit was not just a few hours; it typically meant the visitors would be there for a few days, and that's exactly what happened. They came to stay, and our fishing trip and picnic got canceled to be rescheduled for another day.

After their visitors left town and several days had passed, there was a problem. Our trip and picnic never happened. It was never rescheduled because Pop Paw Counts suddenly got pretty sick. Around that same time my Granddaddy Lucas got really sick and within a very short period of time, both of my grandpa's were diagnosed with cancer. After Granddaddy Lucas got sick, I have memories of going into his room as he sat in a rocking chair by a wood stove to talk to him. I also remember Sunday afternoons when all of us grandkids would be there visiting. We would run in and out of the house, and with each pass in and out of the house, the screen door would slam behind us. Some people wouldn't know what a screen door with a spring is, but I clearly remember them well. I also remember how my Granddaddy would yell out, "DON'T SLAM THE DOOR!" It annoyed him so much, and it didn't bother him to let you know either. I also have memories of sitting by the bed and talking to Pop Paw Counts after he got to the point where he couldn't sit up on his own anymore. While I knew something was happening, I didn't realize how serious things really were.

I can't really remember much about my Granddaddy's passing or his funeral services, but I clearly remember those of Pop Paw Counts. Back in those days, the funeral home would bring the body to the house for viewing. Pop Paw was brought to his house, and he stayed there all night long. I remember that so clearly, and it took me a long time to get over that. Losing both of my grandpas the same year was a horrible thing, and while I was very young at the time, I understood they wouldn't be coming back.

Philippians 1:3—"I thank my God upon every remembrance of you."

Genesis 3:19—"For dust thou art, and unto dust shalt thou return."

A Minute of Meditation

I was very young when I lost my Pop Paw and Granddaddy. Since that time, I've gone down the road of separation many, many times. It's never easy when you lose someone you love, and I learned that far too early in my life. Pause for a minute and thank God for those who were special to you who have gone on. Maybe you can think of a special story or event that took place in your life that involved someone you have lost. You know, these people have contributed to our life in some form or fashion. We are in many ways who we are because of them. Don't allow Satan to silence your memories. Keep them alive by sharing something special that you remember about your loved one with others!

Chapter 3

Time Keeps Marching On

You would think a five-year-old kid wouldn't have memories of things they experienced at such a young age, but I have vivid memories of those years in my life. While some memories are ones we would like to forget, every memory is a part of life that has molded us into the individuals we have become. Good or bad, there's a reason for everything. Why things happen the way they do can't really be explained, other than it's all in God's plan for our lives; we just need to hang on for the ride and place our trust in the God who created us.

By the time I was eight years old, I began to get real curious about heaven and hell and what these places were all about. I was blessed to have been raised in a Christian home. I'm not talking about an Easter and Christmas Christian home, I'm talking about a seven day a week, 365 days a year Christian home! During the summer months, I can remember going to church somewhere pretty much every night of my life. If we didn't attend an ongoing revival service somewhere, we would be attending our home church or watching preaching on the television. It seemed like Billy Graham crusades were constantly being broadcast in our area, and the services would be televised every night. It was just a common practice in our home to watch Billy Graham every time his crusades were televised.

The local Church was very important in the lives of my mother and dad. Here's an example of the weekly service schedule at the little church I grew up in:

- Sunday morning—10:00 a.m. Sunday school

- Sunday evening—7:00 p.m. Sunday evening service

- Wednesday evening—7:00 p.m. Midweek prayer meeting service

- Thursday evening—7:00 p.m. youth service

- Saturday evening—7:00 p.m. fellowship meeting, with a special song service every third Saturday night of each month.

Since Mom and Dad were very involved with the church and served in various positions there, attending was not an option for me. Being the youngest, I couldn't stay home by myself, so they took me right along with them. I sort of think having all the services scheduled the way they were was by specific design—to keep me out of trouble! It was my parents' way of keeping me occupied and out of trouble and harm's way. If they could look back and see me sitting in a church pew, they knew exactly where I was and what I was doing. This left me with little opportunity to get involved in the wrong things that were going on all around us.

In 1972, there was a new television show that aired called *The Waltons*. This quickly became my favorite weekly TV program. The problem was, it came on every Thursday night at 8:00 p.m. This happened to be our weekly scheduled youth service night. I remember getting so upset about this, and I kept complaining about it to the point that youth service was changed to Tuesday evenings instead. Since my mother was the youth director, I convinced her that she had the power to get the day changed in the schedule at the church. Very soon after this, our weekly youth service got changed to Tuesday evenings, and boy, was I happy!

That same year, our church had scheduled a revival service. Back in those days a revival would be scheduled for one week but would often go on and on for weeks at a time. It was not uncommon for the original scheduled week-long meeting to run into three or four weeks long or longer. Well, revival time rolled around, and all the normal weekly services would just roll into revival week and all the events of that particular week were centered around some singing and preaching every night. The revivals were a time for Christians to be "revived" and for Sinners to be "saved." While I was curious about heaven and hell, I wasn't curious enough that I would miss watching *The Waltons* just to find out more about these places. I will never forget that Thursday evening when my sister came walking through the house right about time to go to church. I was sitting in the floor of our living room watching TV, and it was around 7:30 p.m. The revival services would start at 7:30 p.m. to give folks a little extra time to eat dinner after getting home from work and before the meeting would start. Joyce said, "Are you not going to the revival tonight"? My response was, "Are you kidding me, *The Waltons* come on in thirty minutes. I won't be there tonight!" My sister responded on her way out the door with, "Well just die and go to hell, watching *The Waltons.*"

Needless to say, her last comment weighed very heavy on my mind. All I could think about after Joyce left was, I don't want to go to hell. The closer it got to 8:00 p.m., the more I thought about what she said. I decided I needed to go to church, not that I didn't go enough the way it was, I just didn't want to die and go to hell that night there at home all alone. The church was three doors down from our house, so out the door I went, walking to the service.

I slipped in the church and sat down on the back pew. Preacher Arnold Price was just beginning his sermon that evening, and of all things, he was preaching about hell. The longer I sat there, the more I thought that my sister had told Preacher Price about me. The message was God-sent and spot on. It didn't take long for me to get a clear understanding of what hell was going to be like. Preacher Price gave a very detailed description of that awful place, and he also explained that you really don't have to be all that bad to go there. When he said, "All it takes is for you to deny Christ or never accept Him as your personal Savior to end up in hell." That's all it took to get my attention.

I don't remember the exact date on the calendar, but I do remember it was a Thursday night. I really can't remember what I said, but I remember stepping out and walking forward. I know this much: when I knelt down at the altar, I was broken, I was sorry, and I wanted the forgiveness that only Christ could give. I knew I didn't want to go to hell, and if it was really as easy as Preacher Price was saying, I wanted to get it all settled. I heard: you ask, you believe, and you receive, and that is exactly what I did. While I was only eight years old, I sincerely asked God to forgive me, to come into my heart and life, and save me. At that moment, I believe God forgave me and accepted the prayer I offered. His forgiveness was extended to me, and from that day forward, I have never been the same. What a blessing it is to know that a simple act of asking, believing, and receiving is all it takes to reserve your spot in that place called heaven.

Romans 10:13—"For whosoever shall call upon the name of the Lord shall be saved."

A Minute of Meditation

Has there ever been a time in your life when you allowed something to come between you and spending time with God? If you have given your life to Christ, I'm sure you can remember the battle that was raging inside of you the moment God spoke ever so clearly to you, bidding you to come to Him. It's a battle of good against evil. Satan will absolutely use anything to distract us and keep us from asking God to forgive us. He would like to keep you silent about your decision to serve Christ. Don't allow that to happen. I would like to encourage you to share your story with others; don't keep it to yourself! Take a minute and think back to the moment you asked Christ to save you. Thank him for all He's done. If for some reason you don't have that settled in your heart and life, don't let Satan deceive you! Just ask the Lord to forgive you and save you, then tell someone about your decision. You'll be glad you did.

Chapter 4

The War Begins

My life changed the moment I asked God to forgive me. I felt so relieved, like a heavy weight was lifted off of me, and I just knew life was going to be different. I really didn't know how different it would be, as I was young. I hadn't done a lot of bad things, and I didn't have a bunch of bad habits I needed to break; but I knew I needed to be different. I heard the message on hell, and the types of people who were going to be there had been described in that message pretty clearly. While I didn't categorize myself as a whoremonger, a sorcerer, or an idolater, I had lied; and that, my friends, was enough—enough according to the Word of God, for me to end up in that place called hell that was prepared for those described as such. But more importantly, those who are not found in the book of life would be among those who will be cast into that lake of fire for all eternity.

God forgave me the moment I asked Him to forgive me, and that I'm certain of. Life was different for me from that moment on in a lot of positive ways; but I noticed something else that was different. I discovered that it's when one surrenders to Christ that the war begins. Prior to asking God to forgive me, I would describe life as being a series of little battles with the Devil. Nothing huge, just a fight here and there. However, the moment I got down to business with God and asked him to forgive me and save me, that's when life became an all-out war!

You have to understand, I was a very young boy who was right at the beginning of those impressionable years. Living in a home that exercised faith on a daily basis was a major cornerstone for me. I received guidance from the pulpit at church, but more importantly, I received solid, godly guidance from home. I had a mother and a dad who loved God, served God, and shared God with others. They were both committed to our family, and seeing that we were spiritually grounded in our faith was of the upmost importance to the two of them. I'm so thankful for God-fearing parents who loved me and cared enough for me that they wanted to make sure I had the spiritual foundation that was needed to survive in this lost and dying world.

Dad worked as a coal miner but suffered badly with kidney stones, so bad that the company he worked for ruled him as "disabled" and would no longer let him go underground anymore after he had several severe attacks while at work. They felt he would be a danger to the other miners if he should have an attack while operating a piece of equipment, and suddenly, Dad found himself unemployed. Mom no longer worked outside of the home, as Mom Maw and Pop Paw Counts sold the grocery store. Back in those days, the wife typically stayed at home anyway and took care of things around the home, and it was no different at our house. Mom cooked, cleaned, did laundry, pack lunches, and made certain that us kids got off to school and did our homework when we got back home. On top of that, she served and was very involved in the church.

My parents never discussed finances in front of me and my two sisters. I'm sure they both had to be concerned, but if they were, they didn't show it. The decision the coal company had made wasn't going to slow Dad down, he knew how to do other things to generate income, and while he was no longer able to go underground, he worked at building construction and earned a living from that time on as a painter and carpenter. He also knew how to shoot a gun, and I remember him leaving the house many times and coming back with his limit of squirrels that he killed for dinner. I can't think of a time that we ever went without a meal. God always supplied, and Dad would remind Mom of that fact often.

Here in the mountains of West Virginia, mining coal has always been a huge source of income for many families. It was not uncommon for the mines to shut down, leaving many families without a stable income or a way to buy groceries or provide anything that was needed. That's when God's people would kick into action. All the local church congregations would organize a food pounding. Together they would fill up boxloads of food and deliver that food throughout the community to the needy families. While our pantry shelves were pretty bare, Mom and Dad would always contribute and give canned food for the pounding. I couldn't understand it because after they gave, our pantry shelves would have one or two cans of something left on them, and the way I loved to eat, I knew one or two cans wasn't going to go very far. I'm here to tell you, I never missed a meal. Sometimes, one of those boxes showed up on our steps and once again, our pantry was full. God always supplied the need! I witnessed it, and I lived through it, and I'm grateful for a God who cares for His children.

During this time in my life, I started to recognize that my faith was already being challenged. Looking back, I understand that my parents did the best they could do with what they had to do with. As a young boy, I found it hard to understand why things had to be so hard. Money was tight, and I didn't always get everything I wanted. Somehow I felt like Satan was working on me, even in those early years of my life. Those little battles actually turned into an all-out war in my mind, and I've found Satan has never really let up on me since the day I decided to follow Jesus!

Philippians 4:19—"But my God shall supply all your needs according to his riches in glory by Christ Jesus."

A Minute of Meditation

Before we give our life to Christ, there's really no reason for Satan to bother us because he already has control of us. However, when we look to Christ and make the decision that we want Him to be the Lord of our life, that's when Satan starts working overtime on us. It's important to remember who you are serving. When we make a genuine decision to serve God, it doesn't mean Satan is not going to bother us; I think we will have to contend with him until we leave this world, but thanks be to God, the battles are not ours anymore. Take a minute and bow your head and just thank God for the plan of salvation that has been extended to us all. Thank Him for the fact that while it may seem like a war, you know He's a big-enough God who has never lost a battle!

Chapter 5

The Battlefield

Trying to differentiate between "needs" and "wants" can be hard for a young person, and I was no different than anyone else. I had given my life to Christ, and I wanted to be different. However, my definition of different and God's definition of different for me were two very different things! Why should I suffer, why should my family suffer and not have or experience the same things that other people and families experience? As a matter-of-fact, since I am a child of the King, why don't I have the best of everything? I found myself at the point where I was beginning to think that maybe God really didn't care like I thought He should. I had been praying but was not seeing any of my prayers being answered. I had fiery darts flying all around me, and I didn't know how dangerous those darts were. I knew I needed to accept things as they were, but I was not very happy about it. I had to understand that life goes on, right?

I fought this battle in my mind daily for several years. I shared some of the comments that others were saying about me and about our family with my mother, and I know she shared them with my dad. I know this because he asked me about it. Being a proud man, he gave me his opinion of the comments of some of the other kids in our neighborhood, and once again, I was convinced that we were not as poor as some were saying. Dad explained that regardless whether we have the best of everything, we still have what we need. He went on to say we have love and we have Christ in our hearts and in our home, and we have each other. What more could we possibly want or need?

My dad was my hero! So many times, in the short time I was blessed to have him in my life, he came to my rescue. The memories I have of Dad sitting in his chair or at the table, reading his Bible, are forever etched in my mind. The times I heard him stand up in church and testify of God's goodness to him and to our family are anchored in my mind as well. The times I went out on visitation with him and heard him inviting others to church are still with me. I like to think of those moments as being great teaching moments in my life that have stuck with me. His passion for Christ and seeing others come to Christ is something I'm glad I got to see and experience. These moments that I've mentioned are the ammunition I use to remind Satan that, like my dad, I will never give up. I will remain faithful until the Lord calls me home.

This battlefield that I'm talking about consists of a constant war against good and evil. The battle is very real, friends, and I'm writing this to remind you that Satan is very real. He is out to steal, kill, and destroy those of us who claim to be a child of the King. He will rob you of your joy! Satan's ultimate plan is to get us to turn our backs on a God who created us, who loves us, and who has gone to prepare a very special place for us. Let me remind you, the Bible says that eyes have not seen, ears have not heard, and neither has it entered into the heart of man the things God has prepared for those that love Him (1 Cor. 2:9). Why would we ever doubt Him for anything?

In 1978, God called out my dad's name. Apparently his work here on earth was done, and God was satisfied with that. Well, actually, his allotted amount of days that God had for him here on earth was over, and so the dad that I loved dearly was taken away from us. Was I prepared for that moment? Not at all, none of us were prepared for that moment. I'll say this, I know my dad was prepared for that moment. If he had a choice, I think he would have wanted to live here a little longer, but he was prepared to meet Christ, and I have no doubts about that. When this event happened, I will have to say that Satan was doing his very best to silence me. It was not the first attack on my life, but the battle began to rage within me. It was a major battle that I knew would cause me to either get very bitter or it would mold me and make me a better person, but it was very real to me!

Waving the flag of surrender at this time in my life was never an option for me, but I will say Satan can certainly back you up against the wall and make you feel like you have no other options. With my dad now being taken out of my life, I felt as if I was being cheated by God. I began to question God, but the problem was, I was not open to the answers I was getting. I needed to understand that God's ways are not our ways, and for a young teenage boy, understanding God's ways can be a difficult task to say the least. Yes, it is a battlefield, but God will always be with you! God wants us all to have an abundant life, we just need to trust Him!

> John 10:10—"The thief cometh not, but for to steal, and to kill, and to destroy: I come that they may have life, and that they may have it more abundantly."

A Minute of Meditation

Take just a minute to reflect back over your life. Has there ever been a time when you had second thoughts about God? Maybe like me, you felt cheated for some reason or another. Can you remember a specific time when the battle with Satan was so bad that you felt yourself getting bitter over a situation?

Hopefully, you allowed God to have His way and you placed all your trust in Him with the end result being that you grew in your faith, and today you are a better person because of the trial. Pause for a minute and just thank God for never leaving you on the battlefields of your life to walk through those valley's alone.

Chapter 6

Down on My Knees

June 27, 1978 was one day in the history of my life I wish I never had to live through. This was the first year I can ever remember that my dad didn't go on a family vacation with us. My older sister June, her husband, and two kids had moved in with us and were in the beginning stages of building their new home. Dad was going to oversee the construction and decided he wouldn't go on vacation that year. He had a goal in mind of getting the house under roof during the summer months and before bad weather set in so he could work on the interior during the winter months of that year. He insisted that Mom and I go on vacation and enjoy ourselves, but he decided to stay home and keep things rolling along on June's new home.

Mom and I went to Myrtle Beach, South Carolina, with my middle sister Joyce and her husband for our annual beach vacation. It was different as Dad was not with us, but he wanted Mom to go and take me with her so we would at least get a vacation that year. The first mobile phone was invented in 1973, but for the most part, only business people had them. The days of having your phone in your back pocket were nonexistent at that time. As a matter-of-fact, we didn't even have a phone in our motel room. If you wanted to make a call, you typically walked to a pay phone, put money in, and dialed the number for the person you were trying to get in contact with. You could also go to the motel office and place a collect call, which meant the person you were dialing would have to accept the charges related to the call you were placing. How did we ever make it back then?

During the evening of June 26 of that year, we were all out walking along the boardwalk down at the beach. Mom decided she was going to call Dad on a pay phone there at the boardwalk and asked me to go with her to make the call. We had just made it to the local arcade, and I told her to tell Dad hello for me, but I was going in the arcade to play some games. Oh how I wish I could bring back that moment! Mom called and talked to Dad that evening, but little did we know that this would be the last conversation she would have with him this side of heaven.

Very early on the next morning, June 27, 1978, we were all in our motel room asleep when someone started knocking on the door. My brother-in-law got up and went to the door, and upon opening the door, we saw the motel manager standing at the door. I'll never forget this as long as I live. He said, "We have an emergency phone call at the front desk for your party." Our first thought was that something must have happened to Mom Maw Counts; however, when my brother-in-law returned to the room, he broke the news to all of us that Dad had passed away.

I couldn't believe what I was hearing. Dad had gotten up that morning, fixed breakfast, made his coffee, and was getting something out of the refrigerator when my sister June and her husband, Forrest, heard him fall to the floor. They called for help, and the paramedics came as quickly as they could, but it was too late. My dad had a massive heart attack, and his life here on earth was over. Hearing this was so unbelievable for me, and something swelled up inside that I had never experienced ever before. The shock of it all brought on some of the worse feelings within me. Everyone was distraught and wailing with the pain and immediate shock of the news. It was so bad that folks in the neighboring rooms were sticking their heads out of their doors to see what was going on. Suddenly, it was like I was standing in a cloud of unbelief.

Seeing my mother in so much pain was the hardest thing I had ever witnessed. I remember that I was sitting alone on one of the beds crying when one of the maids who worked in the housekeeping department for the motel came over and put her arms around me. She was one of the sweetest black ladies I knew with the voice of an angel. Here I was with a lady I had never met before, holding me in her arms, and both of us were crying like crazy. I remember her saying, "Oh Lord Jesus, help this little boy"! I could tell she knew who Jesus was as that connected immediately with me. It was then that I asked her if she would pray with me. Her response was, "Absolutely"!

I remember looking into this lady's eyes and saying, "I want to kneel down by this bed, please." Together, the two of us began to pray. While I remember the moment, I don't remember exactly what I said other than crying out, "God, help us all"! I wish I knew that woman's name. I sort of feel like she may have been an angel sent there from God up above. I guess it really doesn't matter, but somehow I would love to be able to thank her for being such a comfort to me that morning in my time of need. I hope God will introduce us in heaven one day so I can at least thank her for being the blessing she was to me on one of the worst days of my life.

Friends, in a time like that, Satan seems to have full control over your mind. He started in on me that morning and did his best to convince me that God didn't care about me. He wanted to silence me right there at that very moment, but he only got me down as far as on my knees. It was then that God stepped in and rescued me once again!

Ephesians 3:13–14—"Wherefore I desire that ye faint not at my tribulations for you, which is your glory. For this cause I bow my knees unto the Father of our Lord Jesus Christ."

A Minute of Meditation

Can you think of a dark time in your life when God sent an Angel to minister to your personal needs? I have relived this particular moment in my life over and over now for the past forty-four years. Satan has used this so many times trying to silence me, but I always remind him that through it all, I've survived. Maybe Satan has tried to silence you over a very similar situation in your life. If that's the case, more than likely he brings it to your attention often. Friends, just remind him of how big your God is.

Chapter 7

A Long Road Trip Home

I've been on some pretty long road trips in my life that mileage-wise were a lot longer than the trip home from Myrtle Beach the summer of 1978. I honestly think I cried the entire way while fighting with myself inside as the minutes turned into hours. I was so mad at myself for not taking the opportunity to just go to the pay phone with my mother the night before to call and talk to my dad. What I wouldn't give to have that opportunity again. I was so full of mixed emotions as my eyes were fixed on the clouds that were floating up in the sky that day. How were we going to get through this? Why did this have to happen to us? Why now? These questions just kept surfacing in my mind, but I never received any answers.

It seems like when we are in our weakest moments, that's when Satan works the hardest. At this point in my life, I really didn't know what to do, how to react, even how to respond to what had taken place. Mom was hurting and grieving, so being comforted by her was not an option at that moment. While I understood that we just had to place our trust in God, at my age, I really didn't know what that meant, much less how to go about doing it. Behind the scene, Satan was very much at work on me and in my mind.

In times like these, when we are at our lowest point and in our weakest moments, Satan works overtime. It doesn't take long for him to work his way into the smallest areas of our hearts and minds, and before you know it, he's got you convinced that God has forgotten all about you. Anyone who really knows God would know that God will never leave you. You would also know that He is not going to put more on you than what you are able to carry; 1 Corinthians 10:13 confirms that. Don't get me wrong; sometimes the load gets heavy, and temptations come out of nowhere. However, God will be there for you to help you carry that load. Unfortunately, Satan comes on the scene and goes to work, trying to discourage you, and that's exactly what he was doing to me.

From the time we left the beach all the way home, I had nine hours or so to just sit and think about what I would have to face when I got home. I would not be greeted by my dad. I couldn't even tell him what I had been up to the past few days. I was totally crushed! What would it be like in our home without him? Who would I go hunting and fishing with? I needed a dad, and God had taken him from me. Dad was only fifty-eight years old; that was too young for anyone to die. How could this be? I was beginning to stress out with all the thoughts that were going through my head. Needless to say, Satan never let up; he stayed right after me the whole trip home. Have you ever experienced a time like this in your life? If so, I'm sure you had a million questions in your mind as well. Looking back on this particular situation, I understand now that I'm not the only person who ever went through a battle like this. Softly, God reminded me of my friends who were my age who had died, and this brought things into prospective. Maybe fifty-eight is not so young!

The closer we got to home, the more I cried. Knowing that my dad was not going to be there really bothered me. I couldn't hold back the tears, and I cried so much that I made myself sick. We exited the West Virginia Turnpike and was almost there. Just a few more turns and home was in sight. What a horrible feeling

I had inside as we pulled into the driveway. This place would never be the same! Reality sat deeply in on me when we opened the door and walked into our home. There was an emptiness, a void there that would never be filled. What a horrible time it was.

> Deuteronomy 31:6—"Be strong and of good courage, fear not, nor be afraid, for the Lord thy God, he it is that doth go with thee; he will not fail thee, nor forsake thee."

A Minute of Meditation

When the Lord put it on my heart to write this book, He started dealing with me about how I should put it together. I know I'm not the only person in this world who has experienced or lived through the things that I'm writing about. We've all been there; everyone has had events in their lives that have turned them upside down! Life can be very harsh! Situations arise that are very unexpected. Given the choice, I think all of us would choose not to have to go through these types of experiences. Just in case you've never lost someone who is really close to you; just hold on, it will eventually happen.

Why would I write about all the loss I've experienced? The sole purpose of this book is to get you to see that Satan is trying to silence us all. He will absolutely use anything to cause us to doubt God. If he is successful in causing us to become bitter, then we are very likely to turn our backs on God. Since he knows what his future holds, Satan will always be hard at work, trying his best to destroy us and to rob us of our joy!

Pause for a few minutes and think about your own personal situations that have come up in your past. Look in the rearview mirror of time and reflect on these things for just a minute. Can you see or remember a time when Satan was at work on you?

How did you react? What did you do to win that particular battle in your life? Remember this thought, if you would, and I hope it will help you. The windshield is much bigger than a rear-view mirror in a car. There's a reason for that, and it applies to our lives. God doesn't want us to spend a lot of time focusing on the past. We need to look up ahead and be challenged for the road that awaits us. We've got a great work to do. Don't be silenced by Satan or your past; just keep serving the Lord!

Chapter 8

Emptiness Settles In

When someone dies, it seems there is a never-ending flow of people for days. The house is full, there's a lot of noise, and so much food that you could never eat it all. Everyone who stops by reminds you of what has happened, and while you're trying to get it off of your mind, it's just impossible to do.

You soon find out how important all those people were in the situation. It's when they are all gone that reality sets in. Suddenly, the house is empty, it's quiet again—so quiet that it hurts down deep within to the point that you would give anything to have a few of those folks around just to talk to. I had so much time on my hands, and with each passing day, I found myself getting deeper and deeper in a very depressed state of mind.

My sister and brother-in-law's home was being built just two doors down from our home. The evening after my dad's service, I decided I was going to walk down there to see how far along Dad had got on things while we were gone. He had been working on getting the foundation completed and laying neatly there on his mortar board were the tools he had been using. There was his trowel, tape measure, block hammer, string line, and his jointer tool all laid out in a row. At the end of every work day, Dad would clean up all his tools and have them ready for the next day. He was very particular about his tools, and making sure they were cleaned up was so important to him. If I had been home, he would have had me cleaning them up as that was one of my jobs.

I remember sitting down there on a block and letting my mind wander back to the past few days before Mom and I left for vacation. I reminisced of all the days I had worked alongside my dad on various block jobs he had done, and I could see in my mind's eye him working right there just a few days before. With the tears rolling down my face, I reached over and picked up Dad's tools, one by one, then laying them down in the very order he had them in. I thought about the fact that he was the last person who touched those tools and also how I would never see him holding them ever again. Somehow I had to accept the fact that his work here on earth was done.

I felt so empty inside! So unsure about the future, I really began to question God about all the events of the past few days. I could feel myself getting more bitter by the moment, and before I knew it, I had a lot of major negative thoughts going through my mind. Where do you think those negative thoughts came from? They sure didn't come from God! I found the more I allowed those negative thoughts in, the more negative thoughts I had. As a result, there was nothing positive at all about my life. No matter what I tried, nothing could fill the void that was inside of me.

A few months passed, and soon it was time for me to go back to school. I wasn't at all ready for that, but I knew I had to face the music and get on with my life. How I was going to do it was another story. I was so depressed that I couldn't even think. My grades dropped as I couldn't focus in class, I hated to get out of bed in the mornings, and certainly had no desire to be at school. I missed a lot of school that year, and Mom got really stressed about it. She stayed on me and told me I had to go to school. She even went to the school and talked to the counselor about me to see what she could do to help. I met with the counselor several times and didn't seem to have anything different to share with her. However, she had her input on everything and by the time she finished with me on our last visit, I guess you could say that she got my attention. When she said, "Tony, if you don't snap out of this slump you're in, you are just going to have to repeat this school year." That's all it took! There was no way I was going to add another year to my education. I had enough the way it was, and going an extra year was not an option for me!

We've all heard about or seen the illustration about the half glass of water. We either see it as half full or half empty. At this point, I felt totally empty and couldn't imagine ever feeling full again. My grades were horrible, and I really couldn't see any way of ever digging out of the hole I had gotten myself in. Thank God for the words from my counselor that kept ringing in my ears. I knew I had to get busy. One by one, my teachers started working with me one on one. They would allow me to come into their rooms during my regular study hall times and even during my breaks, and they offered their assistance in an amazing way. Apparently the counselor talked to all of them about my personal situation that happened over the summer, and it was then that they understood what was going on with me. My English teacher, Mrs. Williams, shared that half glass of water illustration with me. She actually had a half glass of water sitting there on her desk. She asked me, "Tony, what do you see here on my desk"? My response was, "A glass of water." She was happy with that answer because she said, "Most people see it as a half-empty glass of water." She went on to say; "You are seeing it as a glass of water, and that is good"! Mrs. Williams told me if I would see my personal situation as an opportunity to improve like I saw this glass of water, then things would certainly change in a positive way for me.

Feeling empty is not a pleasant state of mind to be in. Rather than feeling totally empty or even partially empty, why not look at life in a positive way? Down deep inside of us all, there are positive measures that can make life as positive as we want it to be. Mrs.

Williams convinced me that each individual had to engage the positive thoughts in our minds in order to live a positive life. She was right about that, as I found the more positive I was about things, the better life became for me. Positive vibes generate positive vibes! The same applies to negative vibes; when we allow negative vibes to seep out of us, it affects those around us in a negative way. This was a hard lesson for me to learn. Let me encourage you to be positive in everything you do! Life will be so much better if this becomes a common every day practice for you as well.

Whatever you do, don't allow Satan to silence you when you go through the dark times of life. Remain positive, and live life to the fullest. God wants us to have an abundant life. This means living life in its abounding fullness of joy and strength for our mind, bodies, and our souls. There's no reason to walk around empty! Trust me on that one!

> Ephesians 3:19—"And to know the love of Christ, which passeth knowledge, that ye might be filled with all the fulness of God."

A Minute of Meditation

Can you think of a time when the "Negative Nancy" showed up in you? With the help of my English Teacher, Mrs. Williams, I discovered that a lot of our problems come about because we only see the negative in things. I'm living proof of that. You may have a negative situation that has surfaced in your life recently. Let me encourage you to take a few minutes to think positive thoughts over that situation. The first thing I would suggest is that you think about how *big* the God is that you serve! Even though your glass may only be halfway full of water, if you will see it as a glass of water, you will find that it will at least help quench your thirst if you will drink it.

Chapter 9

Music—A Way of Escape

I grew up going to church and attending every gospel-music singing convention there was around the area where we lived. Just a few years before Dad passed away, he and Mom got me my first bass guitar. I was fascinated by them, probably because every gospel group I heard generally had one. It was an instrument with a deep tone that seemed to be the staple that kept all the other instruments together, music wise. There was a local group that used the church I grew up in for their practice sessions. Since Dad was the Senior Deacon there and since we lived so close to the church, Dad and Mom had a key. Often when this group would need to be let into the church, Dad would have me to run over there with the key to unlock the door for them.

Most of the time, I would sit down and listen to them as they practiced. Their bass player's name was Jim, and he knew I was locked into him as he played every single note. As time went by, Jim would always talk to me, and I finally told him that I wanted to learn how to play a bass guitar one day. He had me to step up there on the stage, and he put his guitar on me, showed me a few notes, and let me play those notes. I was hooked, so hooked that I told Mom and Dad that I wanted to take guitar lessons.

Soon thereafter, I started taking lessons every Monday night at Herbert's Music Store in Charleston. However, there was a big problem. The teacher had asked me what type of music I wanted to play. I told him that I wanted to play gospel music, so he showed up at the next practice session with an old church hymnal. His idea was to teach me how to sight-read the notes and learn how to play by note. It didn't take me long to figure out that this was not going to work. It was a waste of money and time. I explained that I didn't want to learn how to play songs out of a church hymnal; I wanted to be able to play gospel music like I was hearing all the singing groups play that came to our church or played at all the gospel concerts that we attended. I think Mom was at a loss and unsure how to proceed in helping me because I told her and Dad that I just wanted to quit.

Mom talked to a man by the name of Jack Carte who played the bass guitar for another local gospel group. She told him of my desire to learn how to play and asked Jack if he would care to work with me to see if I had any talent and to let her know what she needed to do. Jack was so willing to help. He invited me to come over to his house, and we sat down in the living room and put a gospel album on his stereo. I explained to Jack how the other teacher was trying to get me to play by note. I went on to say that I never saw any bass player who came to our church or at any of the singing conventions with a song book in front of them while they played note for note. Jack explained to me the process of "playing by ear." He showed me a few notes and the process of learning what string and fret to go to when trying to figure out what key a song was being played in. I began working that night on the processes that Jack taught me, and somehow everything just clicked and stuck in my mind.

I spent every spare minute I had in my bedroom, sitting on the bed, working on the art of playing a bass guitar. For hours and hours, I would put on different gospel albums and dream of one day being on a stage somewhere with one of those groups, playing and being a part of something great. Not long after that first visit with Jack, we got together again. He put on an album and had me show him where on the neck of the guitar I needed to be if I was going to play a particular song. Immediately, I found the right key and started to learn what notes to alternate with when playing in that particular key. Jack seemed to be impressed and told me to keep working on it, as he was sure it was going to become a natural thing for me.

I spent hours at a time in my bedroom practicing and perfecting my skills. My dad knew I loved gospel music, but the only place he ever heard me playing was there in my bedroom. Unless God allowed him to listen in from the portals of heaven, he never got to hear me or see me play live with any group. Music became my way of escaping the negative thoughts I had, and it helped me get my mind off of the fact that Dad was no longer with us. I got to the point that I had to put an album on in the morning and play a few tunes before going to school, and I was right back in the bedroom when I got home from school working on what had become my passion. Soon it all started to click, and I felt pretty confident in myself.

Our church always had an all-day meeting and dinner on the grounds every year on Father's Day. My dad lived for this day. As a matter-of-fact, Father's Day of 1978 was the last church service Dad attended before he went to heaven. On Father's Day, 1979, almost a year after Dad passed away, there was a family group from Roanoke, Virginia, who came to sing for the special Father's Day Services at our church. Mom and Dad had all their albums as they sang around in our area a lot back in those days, and they purchased them at other concert venues. I knew every single one of their songs by heart and often put their album on there in my bedroom and played my bass guitar along with them on every song. There was always a break between the morning and afternoon services for lunch. After the members of this group had eaten lunch, they went back inside the church to run over some songs. I went over to listen and told them that I played my guitar with their albums all the time. Their bass player invited me up on the stage to play a few of their songs with them. That afternoon in the service, I was invited to the stage for my very first official debut as a bass player. The regular bass player moved to an electric guitar, and I got to play the bass the rest of the afternoon.

I was as excited as I could be to have been given the opportunity to play that afternoon. After the service, the managing members asked my mom to let me come to Roanoke to live as they wanted me to be a part of their group. My thoughts were, "This will never happen," but God had another plan. Mom talked to me about this, and of course I was ready to go. The next thing I knew, she purchased a plane ticket for me to fly from Charleston, West Virginia, to Roanoke, Virginia, and off I went. Again, this was the summer of 1979, and I really had not thought things through very well at all. A few weeks later, I found myself sitting in a recording studio in Nashville, Tennessee, playing my bass guitar on a brand-new recording this group was putting together. What an opportunity this was for me. I was living in Roanoke, Virginia, working around a lawn mower sales and service shop during the week, traveling every weekend, playing gospel music; and now I'm sitting in Nashville, Tennessee, actually playing on my very first recording project. I thought I had arrived!

During that summer, I was blessed with some great memories and wonderful opportunities. One of the biggest highlights for me that year was when we played at the *Statler Brothers Homecoming* in Staunton, Virginia. Those guys were involved in the country music side of things, but their roots were in gospel music. Every year they had a homecoming concert in their home town of Staunton, Virginia, and gospel music was always featured during their homecoming event at some point. So here I was, a young, fifteen-year-old boy who came out of a little hollow in the mountains of West Virginia, playing in front of a huge crowd of people there in Staunton. What an honor it was to play on the same stage as some of country music's greatest artists, such as the Statler Brothers, Barbara Mandrell, and several other artists that were a part of that great event.

My stay in Roanoke was short-lived. It was my decision, but after praying about things, I felt that my place was to be at home with my mother. I mentioned that I really hadn't thought things out very well and after having a few months to weigh out the good and bad of my situation, I decided I was going back home to West Virginia. I was faced with starting a new school year there in Roanoke and all I could think about were my friends, my family, and especially my mother that I left back home. I was also wrestling with the fact that Mom was home alone, and after everything she had been through, I thought my place was to be with her. I think I upset a few people as we had just recorded a new project, and now I was leaving to go back home, but I felt it was something I needed to do.

I thank God for the opportunity this family gave to me. I was taken in as one of their own, and it was during a time that I was very confused in my life. It was a wonderful opportunity and one I will never forget. The move to Roanoke was the beginning of something wonderful for me and basically set the stage for the rest of my life. Little did I know at that time, though, what kind of an impact music would have in my life. I just knew I had follow my heart as I wanted to make sure that everything I was doing was pleasing to God. So back to the Mountain State it was for me.

Isaiah 13:14—"And it shall be as a chased roe, and as a sheep that no man taketh up: they shall every man turn to his own people, and flee every one into his own land."

A Minute of Meditation

Can you think of a time in your life when you really didn't think things through? Maybe you made a quick decision about something or made a move and soon found out it was just not what you thought it would be. In this particular situation, I was confused, running from problems I had created for myself simply because of all the negative thoughts I allowed in my life. A great lesson I learned was, it is always best to spend time in prayer and simply wait on God! Maybe you have something going on in your life right now that you need to make a decision about. I would like to encourage you by saying: don't rush things and don't do things just because you think it is the right thing to do. Ask God for His input, and wait until you get peace about the answers you receive.

Chapter 10

Home Again

Going back home was something that was constantly on my mind the whole time I was living over in Virginia. I knew for certain that somehow I was going to keep playing gospel music. While I really didn't know how, I just felt in my heart that God had given me the talent, and I wanted to be faithful in using it. Upon returning home, though, I was faced with the emptiness I left behind just a few months before. The feelings I got when I moved back were the same feelings I had when I left for Roanoke. Learning how to ignore the voice of Satan was certainly a challenge for me, and from the very first night back home in my own bed, the battle was raging again in my life.

I was having trouble connecting the dots in my life. You have to remember, at this time I was only fifteen years old, but I was a very confused fifteen-year-old. I was starting to realize that part of our preparation for heaven was a lifetime of warfare with hell. Why I've never been able to rid myself of all the questions I have about the spiritual realm of things is beyond me. I just know it's a constant battle with the devil. From this time in my life to the very day I'm living right now, it has been a constant battle. Is it God's way of refining us? Are we all created as a weak, broken vessel who is always a weak, broken vessel? How are we supposed to figure out God's will for our lives when we are always in a fight with Satan? These are just a few of the questions that

I asked myself so many times and never seemed to ever get any answers to.

It wasn't like I was the Prodigal Son that we read about in Luke 15. I didn't leave home with an attitude; I thought I was leaving to serve the Lord with my music. But I just couldn't get peace about the situation, so I went back home. Knowing that I needed music in my life, I began praying that God would give me direction for my future. The more I prayed, the louder the voice of Satan was in my head. I just about got to the point where Satan was about to win. Once again, he was trying to silence me. I was not finding any encouragement coming from anyone, and I wasn't finding any opportunities much to get out and play music. I was right in the middle of another hard spot in life and wondering why.

Word got out that I was back home in West Virginia, and after several months of just playing my guitar in my bedroom by myself, doors began to open. Unlike today, most groups who went to record a new project back then would take their own musicians into the studio with them, rather than hiring and paying for studio musicians. All at once, I started getting phone calls from local gospel groups who were asking me to play on their recordings. I always enjoyed being in the studio, so I agreed and started working with various groups and playing on their recordings. It kept me out of trouble and also kept me focused on doing something I enjoyed.

My Mom Maw Counts was always an encouragement to me, but she had a different way of going about giving it to you. She knew I was down about something, and one day she asked me to come into her house and drink a coke with her. Her refrigerator was always stocked with ice-cold cokes, and she would have one ready for me every day when I got home from school. Mom Maw lived next door to us, and I loved spending time with her as she meant the world to me. I went in and sat down at the kitchen table and enjoyed that cold coke with her; that was, until she started telling me that I need to learn how to, "be content in whatever state I found myself in." I really wasn't in the mood and didn't want to hear it, so I made an excuse as to why I needed to leave. I'm sure she felt many times that the things she had to say were falling on deaf ears, but actually I heard her loud and clear. The fact is, she normally hit the nail right on the head and was rarely ever wrong about anything.

Things were slowly getting back to some kind of normal. I was back in school, and time was moving on. Mom and I would go to gospel sings every chance we got, and back then, there was pretty much a gospel sing going on somewhere close enough for us to drive to every Saturday night. I really missed climbing on a bus every weekend and heading out to play my music, so my mission to find another group to play for was underway. I think Mom knew I was happy when I was playing music, and she also knew that gospel music was my music of choice. I never had a desire to play anything else and would never even give it a thought.

Soon doors of opportunity were opened to me again, and it wasn't long until I found myself back out there playing music pretty much every weekend of my life. I was satisfied that I was in the center of God's will for my life and wasn't one who wanted to jump around from group to group. I seriously was trying to find my place of contentment in life, just as Mom Maw had recommended; however, it was important to me that I make sure I was doing what I was doing for the right reasons. The sad thing was, I got distracted and allowed my own desires to come before God's desires for me. After traveling with several different groups over a period of several years, I soon realized that everyone was not out there for the right reasons. Confused, unsettled, and very unhappy, I thought it was over for me. I was so confused that I wasn't sure I would ever play music again.

1 Timothy 6:6—"But godliness with contentment is great gain."

A Minute of Meditation

Take a few minutes to reflect back over your life. Think about the times when maybe you felt empty, confused, lonely, and maybe even so low that you felt like quitting. How did you deal with those moments? Did you try to solve your own problems, or did you just give your problems to God and leave them with Him to solve for you?

We should never allow ourselves to get so low that we would even consider giving a thought to giving up on serving God. Every day is not always going to lend itself to happiness. Things are not always going to go the way we think they should go. When we are faced with empty moments, times of confusion, maybe feeling like we are all alone, don't even think about quitting; just think about Jesus. What if He would have called ten thousand angels to come and take him out of the pain He knew He was going to face? What if He decided He was going to abort the mission His Father in heaven sent Him here to do? He didn't quit. My friends, Jesus went all the way to the cross and from there to the grave, but thank God, He defeated death, hell, and the grave, and walked out of the tomb victorious! This alone should be enough to keep us focused and engaged in serving Him all the days of our lives.

Chapter 11

Fast Forward

In late 1982, I was talking to a friend of mine who had been involved in gospel music for a number of years. He asked me why he hadn't been seeing me out in the singing circle. It was just a common thing to run into other groups out and about. We would often be scheduled at the same church or run into each other out at the local restaurants after a service, eating those late-night meals. I explained my situation and told him that I thought I was finished. I had lost my desire to play gospel music or even be involved with it. Being the guy he was, Henry wanted to encourage me. He could tell I was down, so what did he do; he told me he had given my name to a man by the name of Jack Suttle and went on to say, "Jack has been trying to get in touch with you." My response was, "I'm not interested"!

After having had a few bad experiences back to back, I really felt that maybe God was through with me. I had graduated from high school and was working at that time as a welder. I was now thinking about my career and also had other things on my mind—primarily girls. I explained to Henry that I was in search of my soulmate. When I said this, Henry said, "Jack has a daughter!" That got my curiosity up, and I began to think that just maybe I should look into this as it could be that God is connecting the dots for me.

I was technically still in a relationship with another girl; however, things were not going so well. We had gone from romance to fighting every time we were together. My mother was trying to tell me that it wasn't going to work, and of course, I didn't want to hear it. Down deep inside, I knew Mom was right; it wasn't going to work out, and I needed to just move on. I won't spend a lot of time on old relationships, as we've all had them. I'll just say, there were so many crazy events that took place over the next few months of my life that I knew for certain when Lynette and I got together that it had to be a God thing.

Let me back up for just a minute. My friend Henry contacted this man, Jack Suttle, to say he had mentioned him to me and told him that he was talking about his need of a bass player for their family group. The next thing I knew, I received a call from Jack who asked me if I had time for lunch one day. I end up going to lunch with him, as he wanted to tell me about his family and their need for someone to play the bass guitar for their family gospel group. This was late December 1982. Jack invited me to a revival service at their home church that was coming up the first part of January just a few weeks after our lunch. He gave me his phone number and directions to the church and said, "If you decide to come, just give me a call. I would love to introduce you to my family." Over the next several days, I thought about it and just about talked myself out of going all together, but I decided I would take him up on the invitation.

Did I go to this revival service with the right motive in mind? No! I'll be honest about it, I was more interested in seeing what Jack's daughter looked like. Preacher Maze Jackson from Atlanta, Georgia, was preaching the revival, and I will say, he certainly kept my attention. I really enjoyed everything about the service, but after the service, my focus and mission was to meet the family, especially the daughter of the family. Jack's wife Nancy was talking to me after church, and she pointed toward the back of the church and told me where their son Wally was sitting and then she pointed out their daughter Lynette. Wanting to make sure I was looking at the right girl, I asked her for confirmation. She confirmed what I thought she said, and my heart melted right there on the spot. After a few minutes, which felt like an hour, I was meeting Wally and Lynette for the first time.

Jack and Nancy invited me back for the Saturday night revival service and said they had a bass guitar they would bring. Jack said he was thinking that maybe if I was interested, we could run over a few songs after the Saturday evening service. I responded very quickly by saying, "I'll be here." I left the church that Friday evening, and when I walked into the house, my mom asked me how things went. She was certain she knew who Jack and Nancy Suttle were because they had been to our church in the past with another group who was from up around the Clendenin area. I told her things went great, and she was right about who they were. I also went on to say, "Mom, I think I found the girl I'm going to marry!" Knowing my current situation at the time, my mother's response was, "Tony, you are going to kill me, son"!

In my heart, I honestly felt like I had met the girl I would spend the rest of my life with. It took me a while to convince her that I was the one that she would spend the rest of her life with, but I finally won her over. We met in church at a revival service, I fell in love, won her heart, and eventually asked her to marry me. We ended up getting married there at Mt. Pleasant Baptist Church in Elkview, West Virginia, and it has been our home church ever since. Oh, I also made the decision to start playing the bass guitar for the Suttle Family; it was a no-brainer for me!

Psalm 37:5—"Commit thy way unto the Lord; trust also in him; and he shall bring it to pass."

A Minute of Meditation

Has there ever been a time in your life when you knew immediately that God was doing something special for you? While I probably was about to worry my mother to death, she was always my greatest cheerleader! Mom always told me if I would live my life for the Lord that He would give me the desires of my heart. While my motive may not have been what it should have been, God still used the situation to bring the desires of my heart to reality. Satan sure won't do that for you! Had I continued on the road I was on, I'm certain I would have ended up in a failed marriage. If you are not fully trusting God for great things in your life, pause for just a minute and ask Him to help you get yourself focused and where you need to be for Him to bless you like He really wants to bless you!

Chapter 12

Part of the Family

On August 11, 1984, Lynette and I said "I do." Before God, our family, and a host of friends, we shared our vows with each other right there at Mt. Pleasant Baptist Church. I remember when I asked Jack if I could marry Lynette. We wanted his blessings, and I thought for sure he would say yes; however, he threw a little twist in things. His response was, "I sort of felt like this was coming, but I'm going to have to pray about it," and he left it there. Not just a day or two, but a couple of weeks went by, and we still didn't have an answer. He left for a business trip to Texas the day after I asked him and was gone for several days. When he got back, every time I was around him I kept waiting for an answer, but the answer wasn't coming like I thought it should. I asked Lynette if he or her mother had said anything to her about it and suggested that maybe we should ask him again to see what the answer was going to be. Knowing her dad, Lynette said, "Dad prays about everything, and once he gets his answer, he will let us know."

The time finally came when Jack gave us his answer. He said, "Well, I read about all this in the Bible." I said, "You read about me wanting to marry your daughter in the Bible"? Jack goes on to say, "Yes, a man had a daughter, and a guy like you wanted to marry her." He went over the entire story with me about Laban that is found in Genesis 29, starting around verse

16. This man Laban had two daughters. Their names were Leah and Rachel. A boy named Jacob had fallen in love with the younger daughter, Rachel. The Bible says that Rachel was beautiful in form and appearance. (I thought about this, and was thinking so far the story is pretty accurate, Lynette was beautiful in form and appearance!) Then Jack goes on to say that Jacob had agreed to work for Laban for seven years. At the end of the seven years, Jacob asked Laban for his daughter Rachel's hand in marriage, but Laban brought his older daughter Leah before him. Jacob said, this is the wrong daughter and Laban's response was, "You have to work for me another seven years if you want Rachel"! Jack finally said yes, but not before I would agree to work for him for a "very long time"! He said, "I only have one daughter, so I'm expecting it"! This is actually how it went down.

His answer was yes, and the two of us started our life together as one. Both of us had the same desires: we wanted our marriage to be rooted and grounded with God being the center of our home and everything we ever attempted to do. Our pastor at that time, Pastor David Pence, married us, and I think he did a pretty good job at tying the knot up pretty tight. Pastor Pence later told us that we were the only couple he ever married without first counseling them. He said he thought about it, but knew if Jack Suttle had anything to do with us getting married, we had already been given the proper counsel for life.

Shortly after joining the family group as their bass player, one of the nonfamily members who had been singing with them left to go back to singing with his dad and cousins in their family group. Suddenly, Jack came to me and said, "I need you to step it up and start singing with us. Can you do that?" My mom had me singing in church when I was young, and I always sang with the youth group and at Bible Schools I attended as a kid, but I wasn't sure about this. This was actually before Lynette and I were married, and I can say I started to second guess my decision and if this was God's plan for me or not.

I began to struggle with this, and once again, here I was in a battle with the devil. Satan started in on me and was doing his very best to silence me once again. I soon realized how much of a positive motivator Jack Suttle was. I had never really met anyone who was always positive, never had a bad word to say about anybody, and could convince you that you could do anything you set your mind to do, until I met Jack. He just had a way of causing you to reach down deep inside of yourself and find something you can use to help others. Using your talents in a positive way was something everyone could do, and he certainly convinced me of that! This all came up a year or so before I asked Jack to marry Lynette, and I agreed to give it a try. I didn't know if I could sing and play the bass guitar at the same time, but I felt like if I was going to remain a part of this family group, I needed to quickly learn how to get it done. I soon found out that it was like walking and chewing gum at the same time. I thought if I could do that, I could surely play a bass guitar and sing. Actually, I discovered I could chew gum, play a bass guitar, and sing all at the same time. I felt really talented to say the least.

The next thing I knew, we were headed to the studio to record a new album. Jack felt like we needed to learn some new songs and have a new album with those songs on it so we could offer it to those who attended the services we were a part of. It also helped cover the travel expenses involved in a ministry like the family had. I was absolutely a nervous wreck about everything that was going on and didn't know if I could do all of this or not. Somehow we managed to get the project completed, and this was just the beginning.

God blessed the family ministry, and we have so many memories of our days traveling and serving the Lord together. Over the years, God blessed us with buses to travel in, and if you've never spent every weekend of your life and several week-long trips traveling with your in-laws on a forty-foot bus, you should try it. Your faith and patience will certainly be tested, but I would encourage you to just try it! Seriously, it kept us very close, and God gave us so many blessings during this time in our lives.

I could write an entire book about our time on the road, as there are so many stories both good and bad that I could share. I'll say this, it was like Jack would lay a yardstick down on the map and stretch us all to our limits at times. We may be in Ohio one night and find ourselves in Alabama the next. I began to second-guess myself one time when our bus was in the shop, and we had to figure out what we were going to do. A client of Jack's owned a catering business, and the next thing I knew, we were going down to pick up one of his box trucks that he used in his business. The best thing about it was, it smelled like prime rib! The bad thing was, we all smelled like prime rib when we got to where we were going. We loaded all of our sound equipment and instruments in that box truck along with our clothes, bean bag chairs, and folding chairs for some of us to sit in and off we go. It was a bit of an inconvenience, but God was with us, and He supplied exactly what we needed to do what we were scheduled to do.

Lynette and her family had been around the world, serving the Lord. They were blessed to serve in the country of India on several occasions, and Jack was quick to share how God always supplied their every need. After I became a part of the family, God continued to supply our every need. We saw people saved, lives changed, and often received letters in the mail from folks who had been in one of our services, telling us how God had used us to help them see their need of Christ. We ministered pretty much anywhere God opened the doors for us. That meant in churches, tent meetings, civic centers and various concert venues, even inside of prisons right out on loading docks. I remember on one occasion we were scheduled to sing at a lake. It was a hot summer day, and we were told that a stage would be built near the edge of the lake, and folks would pull up in their boats to hear the music. We were the only gospel group that was scheduled at this event, but it was an opportunity to present the gospel. To our surprise, when we arrived, we discovered that the event was sponsored by Budweiser Anheuser-Busch Beer Company and the entire stage area was wrapped with Budweiser banners. I sort of thought this would bother Jack, and I asked him about it before we started pulling our sound equipment out from under the bus to set up. His response was, "We have a job to do; we are going to represent Christ," and that's just what we did.

As any family does, we had our ups and downs. I can honestly say there were a lot more ups than there were downs. Over all the years that we traveled and ministered together, we were blessed to go to so many different places and worship with some wonderful people who became a part of our family and are still our friends to this day. We came off the road several years ago as Jack started having some major health problems. On October 11, 2018, God called him home, and we miss him so much. Through it all, my friends, God has been good!

> 1 Corinthians 3:6, 9—"I have planted, Apollos watered; but God gave the increase" (v. 6). "For we are labourers together with God: ye are God's husbandry, ye are God's building" (v. 9).

A Minute of Meditation

Can you think of a time when things got a little tough in your Christian life? You have to remember, Satan will use moments like this to silence you if he can! When things get rough, we have to get tough. I learned a long time ago that being a Christian doesn't mean everything goes right all the time. Sometimes there are trials, and we are put to the test; however, God uses moments of trials and tests to refine us into a vessel that is usable. Pause and ask God to forgive you for those times you felt like giving up and thank Him for the blessings you received for staying faithful.

Chapter 13

Starting a Family of Our Own

Back in Chapter 1, I wrote about the day when God became so real to me. On September 11, 1988, while standing beside my wife in the delivery room at CAMC Women and Children's Hospital in Charleston, West Virginia; our firstborn son, Zachary Craig Lucas, entered this world. Watching his arrival was such an amazing thing; however, it was when I heard his first cry that I realized just how awesome God really is! Then again on July 21, 1991, at the same hospital; God showed us again how much He loved us as our second son, Parker Jamison Lucas, entered this world. Both times, at the first cry, I never had to wonder if there was a God.

Being raised in a Christian home with a mother and dad who loved and served God was a huge blessing for me. I've met a lot of people over the years who have shared their stories of how they were raised, and when I listen to their stories, I'm reminded of how blessed I was. I really didn't have much choice in the matter, and going to church was not an option for me. Growing up the son or daughters of Cecil and Vivian Lucas meant you would be going to church. Not just some of the time or every now and then, but pretty much all of the time. I didn't always understand it or agree with it, but that's just the way it was. Does this mean that I was raised up a "Christian"? No! It just meant that I had a mother and dad who made Christ the most important part of our family. They valued and had reason to believe that the Bible was and is the inspired Word of God. Their choice of encouraging their children to get an understanding of what living a life based on faith and believing that what this Word had to say was the truth was very important to them. However, their faith was not forced on us. They simply exposed my two sisters and me to the Word of God through the preaching and teaching of the most amazing book there has ever been. The decision to accept the Word and to follow God was a choice that each of us had to make for ourselves. I'm happy to say we have all accepted Christ, and I know my sisters would agree: we are very thankful that our parents cared enough for us that they felt it was important enough for us to get a clear understanding of the truth that will set you free.

For me, becoming a dad was a huge responsibility. I mean, getting married was a major step! Anyone who is married would have to tell you that those first few years are a real challenge anyway you look at it. Two people, two minds, two different attitudes, suddenly are joined together as one. Two individuals who have their own way of thinking and their own way of doing things, all of a sudden have another person telling them just how wrong they are in their thinking and how wrong whatever it is they are trying to do really is! The day I took on a wife and Lynette took me on as her husband was a challenge for both of us, but it was a commitment as well; and sometimes when reality sets in, things can get a little difficult for all parties involved. Once children are brought into the world, though, it's then that you quickly understand exactly what you've done.

In Psalm 127:3–4, we read these words; "Lo, children are a heritage of the Lord: and the fruit of the womb is his reward. As arrows are in the hand of a mighty man; so are children of the youth." I was determined that I wanted a marriage like my mother and dad had. I wanted a wife who had the same spiritual goals that I had, who wanted children, and was willing to commit herself for a lifetime. When we said, "I do," we did, and our boys added a lot of joy and excitement to our lives and have certainly been a blessing! In the same book and chapter of God's Word, Psalm 127, back up in verse 1, it says; "Except the Lord build the house, they labour in vain that build it." What a blessing it is when you and your spouse work together in building a family, a home, and a future, knowing that God has got His hand on you in the process.

Some people are really good at bringing children into the world, but as you look around today, you can see there are a lot of parents who fail to spend very much time with their kids. It amazes me how disrespectful kids and teenagers have gotten. Had I talked to my parents like some of the kids I've heard talking to their parents do today, I would have been walking around with a set of false teeth at a very young age. It's referred to as "abuse" today; but I would have eaten the back of my daddy's hand if I even thought about raising my voice to him or my mother. I enjoy being a father and always have. Once our boys came along, it was just normal for me and Lynette to always have our kids with us pretty much everywhere we went. We cherished every minute we had with them, and believe me, I wish I had another chance to relive those wonderful years.

Just as it was important for my mother and dad to see that I got a clear understanding of what a life in Christ meant, it quickly became a top priority in our home as well. We read parenting books and magazines constantly after becoming new parents. We had never been down that road before; this was the first time, so we wanted to learn as much as we could. When Parker came along, we still had a lot to learn, and as time went on and our boys got older, we realized that it was always going to be a learning process with each new phase that our kids grew into. You can read all the books you want, and I highly recommend you do; however, the most important book you can read and study is the Bible. My friends, there are so many truths found in God's Word that give us great instruction on the right way to raise our children. Whatever you do, don't just bring them into the world and forget about them. Spend time with you kids, teach them right from wrong, live your life in a positive manner, set goals, work hard, and teach your children that working hard is a part of life that will enable them to live a better life. Most importantly, take them to church and sit beside them. Teach them the ways of the Lord, living and leading by example.

I would like to tell you if you do all the things I've written in this chapter about raising kids that you will never have any trouble, but that's just not the truth! I would highly recommend the things I've mentioned, and I really do believe you can't go wrong by taking your kids to church, teaching them about Christ, and living for Christ in front of them. Making sure they hear the Word of God preached and taught from the pulpit, in small youth group settings, Sunday school, Vacation Bible School programs, and AWANA programs is very important; but even though you might do all these things, please know you are not exempt from Satan trying to get in their hearts and minds and taking them down a road of total destruction. You simply have to keep parenting, never giving up, staying engaged, and knowing what is going on and who your children are hanging out with. Get as much of God as you can planted deep within their hearts! More importantly, lean on God for the guidance you're going to need to get them raised.

Zachary and Parker have grown up and are now both raising kids of their own. For the most part, we really didn't have a lot of trouble in those younger years. I think a lot of it is because we were involved in everything our boys ever did. By the time Zachary graduated from high school and made his decision about where he would be attending college; this is when Satan tried his best to defeat me as a dad. After Zach moved out of the house and into the dorm at college, I noticed that he was really beginning to gain his independence. Dad and Mom were not there day in and day out, and while we were still funding most of everything for him, he started to develop an attitude that I did not approve of. He and I began to clash just about every time we were together. It was then that I began to really struggle. I was beginning to see that even though he still depended a lot on us for his financial needs, he didn't see the importance of following any of our rules. I was facing one of the biggest challenges as a dad at that point, and it wasn't pleasant at all.

Looking back on this period of time now, I know and fully understand how much Zachary and I are alike. There are so many of the same characteristics in him that I know for certain I had as a young man myself. I was a protective father by design, and I wanted to be in control, but when I started losing control, that's when the major problems began. Zach and I were both pretty stupid in how we dealt with some of the situations that came up, and I'm not proud of how I reacted at times as his father. Without a doubt, I know I could have done a much better job had I just thought things through a little better. I think Parker learned by his older brother's mistakes and kept his mouth shut, making his life and mine a little easier by the time he made it to his college years. But I'll say, the years between finishing high school and leaving home for college were certainly not a fun time for me.

If God had not been in my life, I'm sure I would have never survived these later years when my kids left for college and while they were getting their college degrees. During that time, Lynette and I were beginning to experience the first phase of those empty-nest moments. That alone was difficult. Suddenly the world starts to influence the kids you love and have invested your life in, and I was just not happy with what I was seeing. Communicating with your own flesh and blood starts to be one of the hardest things you ever tried to do, and guess who starts to work on your mind and spirit? You've got it: Satan! Yes, Satan attacks the best of us and seems to represent himself pretty well. He likes to make you think he doesn't fear the God you say you are serving. The Satan I'm talking about will absolutely get up in the middle of your family in these types of situations, and before you know it, he's trying once again to silence you as a father or a mother! You can't give in; you have to stand strong and realize God is able to take care of every situation.

I thank God for my family and for all the blessings I've experienced with my wife and kids. Through it all, God has been so good to us. Yes, there have been ups and downs, but I'm a blessed man. Overall, the parenting journey has been a wonderful journey. Like an old saying my mother often said, "If you give Satan an inch he will take a mile." If you don't stay involved and engaged in the lives of your children, if you don't make time for them and teach them the ways of the Lord, Satan and the world will step in and teach them the ways of the world, and you're guaranteed to miss out on a lot of blessing!

> Proverbs 22:6—"Train up a child in the way he should go: and when he is old, he will not depart from it.

A Minute of Meditation

If you are a parent of younger children, I certainly don't want this chapter to be any kind of a discouragement to you. As our children grow and develop, things do change. I think it is just a natural progression and the way life is. However, I hope you understand that it's not a bad thing to be involved in your child's life. For those who have lived through this and now have grown kids, I'm sure you can relate to those trying moments and more than likely, you have gone through some major challenges yourself. How did you deal with those times when Satan tried to silence your voice as a parent? We should all exercise patience and think things through a little better before overreacting and building walls that may stand for years between us and our children. Trust God and look to Him for all the answers you will ever need. He definitely knows what is best for every situation!

Chapter 14

Coach versus Dad

From the time my boys were old enough to get involved in sports, we had them involved. The community we live in has always had a great youth sports program. Living close to the local little league baseball field made it really convenient for us. All the kids from around the area generally played and participated, and our boys were no different. Our very first sports experience was with T-ball. Zachary was old enough to go to tryouts, so we took him. It was a situation where every kid that showed up was placed on a team, and all the kids played in every game. The league was huge due to the total number of kids who showed up, so they just kept adding teams. When it was all said and done, there was a shortage of coaches, and somehow I ended up being asked to help out.

Not only was this our first involvement with youth sports, suddenly it was my first coaching job. The only baseball I ever played was sand-lot ball my friends and I organized. As far as coaching went, we made up the rules as we went, and no coaches were involved in our games. While this team was a group of kids who were just old enough to start playing on an organized team, I was doubting my ability to be their coach.

Lynette encouraged me and convinced me that I could do it, and I'm glad she did. I soon found the job to be very fun and rewarding. Our practices brought back a lot of memories from the days when I was a kid, and I have to say, even with all the challenges, I really enjoyed being around all the kids. I also enjoyed spending that time with Zachary. Parker eventually got involved, but baseball never was a passion for him. I was blessed to work my way up through the program and coached them all the way through their little league years on the baseball field.

As time went on, the boys got involved with the youth basketball program in the community, and much like it was with baseball, I found myself learning all the rules of the game of basketball. Once again, I never played on an organized basketball team myself, but I absolutely loved the game. I grew up in the same community that basketball great Jerry West grew up in. I graduated from the same high school that he graduated from, and all of us kids knew who he was. His basketball jersey that was displayed in our schools gymnasium inspired a lot of us boys in the community. I think we all probably dreamed of being a basketball great like Jerry West, but having the talent he had was something else. I always had a basketball hoop in my yard and spent a lot of time there shooting baskets, but I was not fortunate enough to have a dad who encouraged sports involvement in our home. Dad enjoyed watching baseball on TV, but I can never remember a time that he ever went to a live sporting event. It just wasn't important to him.

Shortly after the boys got involved with the youth basketball program, o'l Dad was right back at it, and once again, I found myself sitting on the sidelines as their coach. I saw talent in Zachary and Parker early on, and fortunately, I got paired up with another gentleman who lived in our town who didn't have a dog in the fight. Mr. Dave Fields was a retired military veteran who played on the Air Force Military Basketball Team and traveled around the world, playing basketball. He didn't have any kids or grandkids involved in the program, but Dave loved working with kids. I was blessed to be able to coach with Dave, as he taught me so much about the fundamentals of the game, and my boys greatly benefited from his teaching and coaching of the game.

God blessed me and allowed me to coach my boys all the way from the early days of the youth basketball program, right on up through the Middle School years, in the AAU sports program, and even through high school. They both worked very hard on their game, and their natural talents gave them a lot of opportunity. For me, the journey through the various programs brought with it a lot of personal satisfaction and enjoyment. While I was able to spend countless hours with my boys, it was great to have the opportunity to just be there for them and have a small part in their personal accomplishments. Together, we experienced undefeated seasons, won state championships in AAU and went on to play in the National AAU Tournament, with our team defeating a Tennessee AAU Team that was coached by coaching legend, Ms. Pat Summit. These are great memories that I dearly cherish!

Coaching your kids can be both a blessing and a curse. I always considered it a blessing; however, there were times when I'm sure my boys would have liked to have had someone else for their coach. It started with T-ball and advanced all the way through their high school years. I was on the sidelines of the football and soccer fields, in the dugout at the baseball field, and on the bench as their basketball coach at the gym. There were never any exceptions made for Zach and Parker just because they were my kids, and they knew this. As a matter-of-fact, I was probably harder on them than I was on all the other team members. They put in the time and worked hard on their game, and it always showed up on the field and on the court. With a genuine love for the game and a true competitive spirit, we all found that the sky was the limit.

One of the biggest problems I think a lot of parents have is when they get so involved in their kid's lives that they want to live out the things they once may have dreamed of doing themselves through their kids. I'm sure I coached some kids who hated me. For the most part though, I would have to say I connected well with all of the kids I ever coached. They knew I was committed to being the best I could be for them. I know I expected a lot out of them, but I always tried to encourage them in the process. My goal every season was to see improvement in every player from the beginning to the end of each season. You always have to deal with some kids who are simply a pain, but if they were a part of any team I ever coached, they knew they would not be a pain for long.

I'm here to tell you, as a coach who is also the father of one or more of the players on the team; there is no way humanly possible that you are going to please everyone. I could deal with the attitudes of the kids, and we always worked through any problems we had together for the most part. However, the parents are a different story! Even during the undefeated seasons, there is always someone who is not going to be happy. Not only does it make things hard for you as a coach, but it's hard on your kids as they hear more than they need to hear and far too often they get the blunt end of the situation, which is not fair at all to them. It takes an awful lot of patience to be a coach and dad at the same time, and I really lacked patience in those days. More often than not, I had to remind my boys that when we are at the field or in the gym, I was coach; and when we got in the car and headed home, I was dad. That, my friends, can be a very confusing thing for a young mind.

Zachary went on to played college basketball, and Parker was recruited by WVU and had a very promising future there until he had a heat-stroke one day during practice at the Coliseum. I'll never forget the phone call I received from the basketball office that day. My cell phone was ringing and when I answered, the voice on the other end said; "Mr. Lucas, this is the secretary in the basketball offices at the University. I was asked to give you a call. Please sir, don't be alarmed, but something happened to your son Parker during practice today." I was told that Parker had to be rushed to the University Hospital as he collapsed in practice. They couldn't tell us much about the situation, but assured me that they would stay with him there at the hospital until we got there. All I could think about was those words, *"Don't be alarmed"*! Are you kidding me? How could I not be alarmed? Plus, I had to tell Lynette that our son was rushed to the University Hospital and we needed to head to Morgantown. I knew this would be a very hard thing to do, but somehow we held it together as we jumped in the car and headed out.

We didn't have a private plane, but our car was flying low on its way up I-79 north from home to Morgantown. It's approximately 140 miles, and the trip normally takes around two hours and fifteen minutes. I prayed all the way that God would make sure there were no police out, as a ticket was the last thing I needed to deal with. One hour and twenty minutes later, we were walking into the hospital. The Lord got us there safe and certainly in record time!

When we arrived at the hospital and walked into Parker's room, I'll have to say, it was a very scary time. Parker was able to talk to us, but he really didn't have a clue what had happened to him. The team trainer explained what took place and what they did for him, but he was very concerned for Parker and said he was definitely where he needed to be. By this time, several doctors had already been in as they were trying to assess the situation. Minutes turned into hours, and we lost count of the number of doctors who came in the room to talk to us about Parker's condition. It was not until the next day that we were told that Parker had suffered a heat stroke. How could this be? Parker had never had a problem like this before. He played full soccer games from start to finish with only a halftime break. He played four full quarters of basketball with only time outs and a halftime break so many times. Why was this happening?

Zachary received scholarship money for basketball and that helped us so much with his college tuition. I knew that Parker had the talent and ability to get the same financial help, but suddenly things were not looking so good. While trying to encourage Parker, I guess I became pretty selfish about the situation. Here he was laying in a hospital bed and I'm telling him that everything is going to be okay when I really didn't know if things would be okay or not. Was I concerned about Parker's medical situation? Absolutely! Was I concerned about how this was going to affect his future with the university basketball team, absolutely! I was really overwhelmed about everything, and Parker said, "Dad, I'm done!" I spent the next several hours trying to convince him that he was not done. It was then that Parker told me that I needed to quit trying to live out my dreams through him.

I'm honest when I say this, but I never had a dream to play college basketball. I never had a dream of playing much of anything as I really didn't have much confidence in myself and also didn't have the support of my parents when I tried playing sports. It was never something that I wanted for myself, but I was very excited to see where the opportunity was going to take Parker. There was never a doubt in my mind that he would make a great college basketball player. During the summer between his senior year of high school and his freshman year at WVU, I attended a lot of the team practices in Morgantown. Never once did I doubt that he was going to be a great asset to the team. But the things Parker told me that day crushed me! It cut me so deep to think that he thought I was trying to live out a dream of mine through him!

The situation with Parker could have been so much worse than it was. The risk of injury and even death is a common thing these days with athletes. Career-ending injuries happen in every sport, but far too often, life-ending events take place. We had a local high school student and football player to collapse and die this year while playing a game in a neighboring community. I understood then how serious it was for Parker, and while I wanted to see him play in college, I wasn't going to force him to do anything that he was not comfortable doing. I certainly didn't want to encourage him to work through the situation and see him die as a result of some kind of hidden health condition that we were not aware of. So the decision was made, and it was final, Parker decided he didn't want to take any chances, and his mother and I fully supported him in his decision.

Once Parker made his decision, Satan got all over me. I prayed and prayed about my attitude and wanted Parker to understand that I backed him and totally understood his decision for doing what he did. Somehow, I never felt that I could get him to believe me. As a result, Satan slipped in and was trying his best to drive a wedge in between me and my son. I couldn't allow that to happen, but once again, the devil was hard at work on me. My friends, he will do the same to you if you're not careful. Failure to realize that there is a problem early on in a situation could result in a lifetime of being disconnected from your own flesh and blood. Would Satan actually do that? You bet he would!

If you ever have an opportunity and are fortunate enough to coach you kids, by all means, do it. Keep in mind, though; those days are limited. At some point, the window for your kids to play baseball, soccer, basketball, football, or any other sport will pass. Your voice as a coach is one thing, and it's important that the players on your team know how to take you and how to respond to what you're asking them to do. This includes you own kids. More importantly, your voice as a parent needs to offer positive reinforcement, vocalized compassion, and you always need to be supportive to your children. Whatever you do, don't allow Satan to use a situation to silence the communication between you and your children! It's just not worth it, and you will regret it. Furthermore, life is too short for things like this. Support your kids and their decisions and love them in the process. You will be glad you did!

> James 4:14–16—"Whereas ye know not what shall be on the morrow. For what is your life? It is even a vapour, that appeareth for a little time, and then vanisheth away. For that ye ought to say, If the Lord will, we shall live, and do this, or that. But now ye rejoice in your boastings: all such rejoicing is evil."

A Minute of Meditation

In situations like I've written about in this chapter, I would recommend that you not allow yourself and your particular desires for your kids to get in the way of what God may want for their lives. Nothing is worth your child losing their life or suffering with a major health condition that they will have to live with the rest of their lives. Be supportive and look to God for answers and direction in every unexpected circumstance. Can you think of a time when you actually wanted something for your child possibly more than what they wanted it? Have you ever been selfish or too demanding, requiring maybe more than what your child is able to do or give? Just remember, "Life is but a vapor"!

Chapter 15

Double-minded

Sometimes life can be confusing at best. It's demanding and stressful, and things can get very complicated in a hurry. Society in general has so many ideas and opinions about what we need to do in order to live a happy and successful life. Those ideas get thrown at us from every direction and often come from our spouses, friends, employers, family members, and sometimes from a complete stranger. Our thoughts and minds get consumed with all the different suggestions about how we should live, how we can make more money, how we can live a healthier and happier life with less stress, and on and on it goes.

Social media seems to have taken over the minds of a lot of people. There's so much knowledge available to us today. Our children are being educated through the internet, and even we adults can gain a lot of knowledge from that particular source of technology. We are simply bombarded with knowledge. I'll admit, it's great to have so much information readily available and right at our fingertips. However, it can be a very dangerous thing as well.

It's important for us to understand, though, that everything we hear or read is not necessarily the truth. Rather than taking what the internet says success is as the gospel, why don't we spend more time in God's Word to find out what it has to say about success? After all, the Bible is a book that was inspired by God, the Creator of it all. The stories we read about in that amazing book are stories of old that give us insight on the great miracles that were performed right in front of the eyes of the people who wrote about them. The writers, who were inspired to pen the words we now read, lived through and witnessed many of the things that were recorded and have been preserved throughout the ages. These things were preserved for us today. Over and over again, throughout history, the Word has been preached, and people have experienced life-changing events through faith and in believing in the God who was and is and is to come.

Just about everything you buy today comes with a set of instructions. If for some reason the instructions are not included with an item you buy, you can google that item on the computer and pretty much find out anything you want or need to know about it. Life is much like that. The Bible was written and pre-pared as an instruction book for us all. I believe it's one of the greatest books ever written and has been America's best seller over and over again. Some people don't read or follow instruc-tions at all. They try to put things together on their own and always seem to have left-over parts. These same people who don't read or follow basic instructions most likely don't read and follow the instructions that are found in God's Word. Not only do they have a lot of screws, nuts, bolts, and washers left over to keep as a special treasure for another project down the road, their life ends up missing the necessary parts that are needed to live the abundant and fulfilled life that God wants us all to live. Things start falling apart and are just not as secure as they should be, and they can't seem to figure out why that is.

A pastor friend of mine, who I was blessed to spend a lot of time with, seemed to always know when I was struggling with something related to the spiritual side of life. He had been around the block a time or two and had a lot more ministry experience than I do. For the most part, I enjoyed spending time with him and serving the Lord right beside of him; however, it was when he started preaching to me that my struggles seems to intensify. He was generally spot on with what he was telling me, but as most people do, I found myself wanting to run from the truth.

After being involved in the family ministry for years and suddenly finding ourselves no longer doing that, it became easier to get involved in other things that I had never had the opportunity to do. My boys were interested in playing travel ball, and doors opened for that to happen, but the problem was it took me in a different direction, and I quickly became distracted. God had been moving in my life and speaking to my heart in a lot of ways, but I wasn't listening very well to His voice. The fact is, I kept myself so involved in other things that ministry was put on the back burner, so to speak. While I knew I was making a mistake, I still pressed on, and by turning down the volume on the voice of God, the voice of Satan became much easier to hear.

I thank God for all the spiritually grounded people He has placed in my life. I'm talking about people like my pastor friend I just mentioned. Having gone through a lot of the same battles I was going through made it much easier for him to give me very sound, godly counsel. Some of the stories and experiences he shared with me about his personal struggles early on in his ministry seem to resonate powerfully in comparison to a lot of things I was going through. God knew I needed to hear these stories, and it was good for me to see that even great men, who have followed God a lot longer than I have, experience trials. The many conversations I had with this faithful brother-in-Christ taught me that the trials we experience today help us to minister to others tomorrow.

I've heard a lot of people talk about how they ran from the voice of God. I'm here to tell you, it's not a pleasant thing to do. Why do we run from a God who loves us and wants the very best for us? That still, small voice that speaks to us is a very distinct voice. It calls us to salvation, it calls us to serve, and it calls us to stand firm in our faith, yet we run from that voice. Why is that? Well it's primarily because the volume of the voice of Satan tends to be much louder, and rather than turning the volume down on Satan, we fall into his trap. Satan chimes in and does what he can to distract us, discourage us, and even send us on a detour, all in an effort to silence us.

You just can't serve two masters! You either hate one and love the other, but God is not going to play second fiddle in your life. Let me say, God is not at all forceful. He gives us all the freedom of choice. Does He care that some choose to listen to the voice of Satan and follow him? Of course He cares! That's why He sent His only son to fulfill the need of a pure and spotless sacrifice for sin. Think about this for a minute. The God who created the world and everything in it apparently was man enough and smart enough to realize that His initial plan was in danger of falling apart. Before He let that happen and because of His love for what He had created, He made a way for us all to avoid the eternal penalty of *sin*. This is where His Son Jesus came on the scene and why the story of His life is so important for us to know and understand. Friends, you don't want to miss this! It's really pretty simple. You listen to and follow Satan's guidance through this world, and you will end up in a place called *hell*; or you can listen to and follow God and experience eternal life in a place called *heaven*. There's a drastic difference between the two places, and for me, it's a no brainer!

When we turn away from God, we are letting God know what our choice is. It's not like He doesn't know it, but He's kind enough to let us hang ourselves. As I just said in the last paragraph, "God is not at all forceful." He is not going to force on us all the wonderful things He has created for us! It's really easy to see when someone is struggling with something. For my pastor friend, it was very easy for him to see my struggles because he had faced a lot of those same struggles early on in his ministry. I'm thankful that he was faithful to stay after me and to continue offering the encouragement I needed for my journey. While it may have taken me a little longer to get a clear understanding of what he kept saying to me, finally one day the light came on in my head. The sad part about it for me is, I wandered around for far too long, thirsting for something special from God. I was living below the level of blessings He wanted for my life and all because I was double-minded.

> Matthew 6:24—"No man can serve two masters; for either he will hate the one, and love the other; or else he will hold to the one, and despise the other. Ye cannot serve God and mammon."

> James 1:8—"A double minded man is unstable in all his ways."

A Minute of Meditation

Has there ever been a time while on your spiritual journey when you seemed to be very confused? You are a saved Christ follower, you know the voice of God, and you know what it is that you are supposed to do; yet you've been walking around in the fog and just can't seem to figure out why. Does this sound familiar to you? Friends, when we know we need to be involved in God's work, but the things of this world seem to be more important, that is a definition of someone who is double-minded! We should let the two verses I've shared at the end of this chapter speak to us daily. These verses remind us that we need to turn our focus toward God and the things that matter the most to Him. Trying to please two masters is just impossible!

Chapter 16

Three Questions That Changed My Life Forever

During all those years that I traveled and was involved in the music ministry, over thirty years in all, God had been dealing with me for a long time about surrendering to the call to preach. I had so many conversations with God about this that I couldn't count them. I would take two steps forward and five steps backward with one excuse after another as to why I couldn't do what He was asking me to do. Fear settled in, and we all know where that comes from, but I trembled at the thought. However, I knew it was God speaking as He never quit calling.

Getting on a stage with hundreds or thousands of people out in the audience was not a problem for me as long as I had my family or others up there with me. But I had a problem with the thought that it was just me up there with nobody around me for support. I always hated it when I was in school and had to get up in front of my class and speak, so in my mind, I knew it was not going to be any different if I got up in front of a bunch of people to preach. The thoughts of it made me nervous. I thank God though for opportunities to preach and share God's Word with others, but Satan never lets up on me!

Our family came off the road with the family ministry, and I'll be very honest with you, I got pretty lazy. I had been so used to climbing on a bus every weekend of my life after working all week and basically working all weekend in the ministry. Imagine working seven days a week, pretty much fifty weeks out of the year and often mixing family vacations with revival meetings during the evening hours of vacation, and doing that for thirty-plus years. Then suddenly, all that stops and you find yourself sitting at home kicked back in the easy chair doing something you've never really had the opportunity to do. I'm telling you, it will make you *lazy*!

We were attending our home church on a regular basis, which is something we never really did on the weekends because we were always on the road serving in other churches. Our home church would basically have us to put a service down on our calendar and schedule us to sing just like any other church would, and that was primarily when we attended there on the weekends. But other than that, Wednesday evening midweek services were about all we would ever get to attend. There was a man in our church by the name of James Chance Steed who was totally full of God from the top of his head all the way down to the bottom of his feet. For several years when I first started attending Mt. Pleasant Baptist Church, Jim was the bus director there at our home church. He and his wife never had any children of their own, so all the bus kids that were brought in to church on the buses became Jim's children. Jim was one of the happiest people I guess I've ever met. He always had a smile on his face and was a faithful servant of God for many years.

Jim and his wife supported our family ministry for years, both financially and prayerfully. If Jim told you he was praying for you, you could take that to the bank, as you knew he was praying for you! When he started seeing us at church on a regular basis on Sundays, he finally came over and asked if we were no longer traveling like we did. I explained that we had slowed down and because of what the doctors had told my father-in-law about his health issues that we had made a decision to come off the road. This seemed to kindle some coals deep down inside of Jim. It was not long after I explained all this to Jim that I noticed he would track me down either before or after every service. If he didn't catch me inside the church, he would make it a point to run me down on the parking lot before getting in my car as he had a mission on his mind.

In 2011, Jim turned the heat up on me. You see, he had been traveling and ministering out in the fairs and festivals of America for several years himself. He was now seventy-five years old and had some medical problems of his own, but he was pleading for help with his ministry. He asked me several times in the past to go out with him sometime just to see what it was all about, but I just kept making excuses as to why I couldn't do that. His come-back was always, "Just pray about it," and my response would be, "I will." And I thought that would be it.

Jim never let up. It was like he had the crosshairs of a scope on me, and I was his target. I finally went from telling him that I would pray about it to saying; "Jim, it's obvious that you think God is speaking to you and telling you that I need to step up and help you with this ministry, but you need to pray that God will show me that this is what He wants me to do." He said, "You've been praying about this for years now, but I don't have a problem asking God to get your attention, boy"! I didn't have to wonder if Jim would call out to God on my behalf or not; I just knew he would and he did! My concern after that statement was, how or what was God going to do to get my attention?

Around the middle of May, 2011, Jim and I had lunch together in downtown Charleston, West Virginia. I want you to know, this man had a heart for the souls or men, women, boys, and girls. It was his desire above everything to point people to Jesus and do whatever he could to help them see their need of God in their lives. Jim always used a little smiley face gospel tract to break the ice with people, and he could start up a conversation with anyone, as he never met a stranger. On the front of the little tract, was a bright yellow smiley face with the words that said, "Smile Jesus Loves You." Across Jim's face, there was always this contagious smile that everyone who looked his way had coming right back at them. If he said anything to you, you couldn't help but stop and talk to him, and all this made him a very special individual.

Over lunch that day, it was almost like Jim knew something that nobody else knew. Once again, he was pleading with me to help him out. He had some upcoming events that were within driving distance of my home, and he invited me to come out and just see what it was all about. He explained his setup with me, but mentioned that at the age of seventy-five, he was running out of juice and he could use the help. He went on to tell me that he really was looking for someone to step in for him as he felt as if maybe he was getting too old to keep up the pace. I could see where the conversation was going, and while Jim was talking to me, Satan was up on my shoulder screaming in my ear, already telling me that I couldn't do this.

Within a few minutes, Jim pulled out one of those smiley tracts and extended it over to the guy who was sitting there in the restaurant at the table beside of us. The conversation between Jim and this stranger was well underway, and here I was sitting there taking all of this in. Jim was not forceful and he didn't push anything on the other man, he was just smiling and talking, all the while he was pulling information out of the guy, and I really don't think the man even knew what was happening until their conversation was over. Through that conversation, Jim showed me just how easy it was to witness to another person and share the goodness of God with them while planting good spiritual seeds they will take with them as they walk away. More importantly, Jim let me in on something very special. He helped me to realize that when we use our voice for the Lord, many times someone else has already planted a seed, it's been watered, and their hearts have already been prepared for us to enjoy the blessing of seeing them make a commitment to follow Jesus.

> Jesus saith unto them, My meat is to do the will of him that sent me, and to finish his work. Say not ye, There are yet four months, and then cometh the harvest? behold, I say unto you, Lift up your eyes, and look on the fields; for they are white already to harvest. And he that reapeth receiveth wages, and gathereth fruit unto life eternal: that both he that soweth and he that reapeth may rejoice together. And herein is that saying true, One soweth, and another reapeth. I sent you to reap that whereon ye bestowed no labour: other men labored, and ye are entered into their labors. (John 4:34–38)

Jim's attention switched back over to me and he said, "Did you see how simple and easy that was"? Then he asked me three questions that I have never forgotten. He said, "Tony, let me ask you, son, *what are you doing for Christ, where are you going for Christ, and who are you taking with you on your journey to heaven?*" I had never had anyone ask me those questions before, but I'll tell you, these questions sure made me think about how lazy I had become and how little I was doing for the cause of Christ.

Lunch was over and we got up and walked out to our cars. On the way out, once again, Jim invited me to come out to the fair he mentioned that was coming up. I told him once again that God was going to need to show me that this is what He wanted me to do, and I promised Jim that when He does, I'd give it a try. Jim assured me that he was going to ask God to show me because in his heart, he could see that I had what it takes to reach others with the gospel of Christ.

I would be lying if I told you I didn't struggle with all that had just happened. I lost a lot of sleep over that conversation, and there were a lot of nights that I kept Lynette awake as I tossed and turned in the bed with restlessness over Jim's plea with me. While I did pray about it, the devil certainly wasn't letting up on me. As a matter-of-fact, he had me seriously believing that I couldn't do what Jim did. I could talk to people with no problem, and I knew that, but Satan had me convinced that this was not for me. On top of the questions Jim had presented to me the questions What are you doing, where are you going, who are you taking with you with you to heaven when you leave here, Satan was asking me a bunch of "What if" questions (What if you make somebody mad? What if you are unable to remember the scriptures? What if you are confronted by an unbeliever who challenges you with the scriptures and you can't think fast enough to get yourself out of that mess?). What if, what if, what if?

It was Memorial Day weekend, Monday, May 30, 2011, just a few weeks after my lunch that day with Jim. Our oldest son Zachary would be graduating from college soon, and we had a lot of family in visiting for the long Memorial Day weekend. Lynette and I decided it would be a good time to have a cookout and a family gathering to celebrate Zach's accomplishments. Due to the number of people who were planning on attending, we had asked our pastor if we could use the gym behind our church as a place for the family to come together for the day. It was supposed to be a very hot day, and we thought it might be nice if we could just have the dinner inside the gym as it was air conditioned and would be a much cooler setting, especially for those who were older in the family. Nothing was on the schedule for that day, so this worked out great.

Zachary helped me load grills and coolers in the truck, and we left the house to go down to the gym a little early to set up tables and chairs and to also get the food on the grills so everything would be ready when everyone arrived. I pulled up to the front of the gym and let Zach out so he could unlock the main doors and come through to the side and open things up as we were planning on cooking out beside the gym. Looking up I saw our pastor's wife taking a bag of trash over to the dumpster, she waved and disappeared around the corner of the gym. Suddenly, she comes running and screaming, "Help, Tony, come and help"!

There are parts of the next hour or so that are a blur to me, but for the most part I will never forget what took place. Jim had his motorhome parked out beside the gym and was washing it getting ready to leave out for another fair. Again, this was a very *hot* Memorial Day, and one of the men of our church has been there just minutes before helping him, but he left to go to a family function that he and his family were having. Jim told him he just had the windshields to finish, and he would get that. When I pulled my truck around the corner of the gym, there was Jim laying on the ground in front of his motor home. Anita had 911 on the phone as I jumped out of my truck. I couldn't feel a pulse at all; Anita told me the ambulance had been dispatched and was on its way, and then she handed me the phone. The guy on the other end asked me if I could at least start CPR on Jim. I explained that it had been years since I had taken a class, but I was willing to do whatever I could to help if he would give me instructions over the phone. With the phone put on speaker, Anita and I proceeded to do CPR. She was doing the compressions, and I was blowing air into Jim's lungs. We could never get a pulse.

The paramedics arrived and quickly took over. I had a pair of shorts on and was down on my knees in the gravel there on the parking lot with gravel embedded in my knees. I continued to do what I could, but Jim had already made his trip to heaven right there in front of us. I was as broken as I could be. I lost my dad to a heart attack, and all that had taken place was just about too much for me to handle. I stood up and stuck to my knee was a gospel tract that said, "You're Invited to Mt. Pleasant Baptist Church." Lying on the ground beside Jim was one of those "Smile Jesus Loves You" tracts that Jim used that day at lunch just a few weeks before. Here was a man out washing his motorhome on a very hot day with his shirt pocket and his pants pockets full of gospel tracts. He was always prepared to witness and did so even in death.

I've referred to this event as my burning bush experience since that day. If there was ever a time that God spoke to my heart, it was on May 30, 2011. Right then and there, just like God spoke to Moses out of the burning bush, He spoke to me! I immediately thought of the story of how Elijah passed his mantle to Elisha, and I knew that Jim's prayers had been answered and confirmed in my heart that very moment. Those three questions that Jim asked me were ringing in my ears louder than ever. How could I ever deny that this was not meant to be?

> 1 Kings 19:19—"So he departed thence, and found Elisha the son of Shaphat, who was plowing with twelve yoke of oxen before him, and he with the twelfth: and Elijah passed by him, and cast his mantle upon him."

A Minute of Meditation

How do we recognize when God is speaking directly to us? Well, He often speaks through others. Sometimes various circumstances and things we go through are God's way of speaking to our hearts and giving us direction for our lives. When things fall into place and specific events take place that give you the assurance that God has heard and answered your prayers, my friends, it's time you pay attention! God's plan and purpose for our lives can be difficult to see and understand at times, but when things stack up the way they did for me in this instance, it's useless to keep running. Just surrender and do whatever it is that God is asking you to do. Maybe you need to pause for a minute and ask yourself those three questions that Jim asked me that day over lunch. Give some thought to what you are currently doing for Christ, where are you going in your Christian life, most importantly, who are reaching out to for Christ with the truth that will set them free? Ask God to show you how you can contribute to His cause.

Chapter 17

Taking a Step of Faith

I'm not sure why this is, but after Jim's passing and through his death, it seemed all those conversations we had were sounding off louder than ever before in my head. The battle with the devil got stronger and harder than ever as well. Now that Jim was gone, I was thinking I was off the hook with this fair ministry idea he had thrown at me, but God had another plan.

While attending the funeral services of my friend and this great man of God, John Gardner with Amazing Grace Missions spoke and shared insight about the mission work Jim had been telling me about. He told of all the reports that Jim had sent in over the years of all the people he had introduced to Christ, who had accepted Christ in their lives because of his faithfulness. What an amazing tribute it was for Jim that day, and once again I found that God was speaking to my heart about all the things Jim and I had discussed over the years and as recent as the past few weeks.

After Jim's homegoing service, I introduced myself to Mr. Gardner and told him how much I enjoyed everything he shared about Jim and the ministry of Amazing Grace Missions. I explained to him that Jim had been talking to me about the fair ministry that he had been involved in for several years and when I did, Mr. Gardner said, "So you are the guy Jim has been talking to me about." Needless to say, Satan suddenly jumped right up on my shoulder and said; "Oh no, here we go again"! The next thing I know Mr. Gardner is asking me for my phone number and wanted to know if he could call me sometime. As I'm driving off the parking lot, all I could think about was, "How in the world am I ever going to be able to get out of this"?

Over the next few weeks, I was totally restless. All the events that had taken place in my life in recent days were absolutely driving me crazy. The thoughts of stepping up and stepping out in faith were actually sort of haunting me. Is this really how God works? I couldn't sleep, during the day I was restless and always nervous, over and over I could hear the voice of Jim in my head, and now it was louder than it had ever been. How was I going to deal with this? I had pretty much convinced myself that there was no way possible that I could ever do what Jim was doing. After all, he was retired, he traveled around in a motorhome that he stayed in at the location of the fairs he worked in, and I knew I couldn't afford to buy a motorhome. As a matter-of-fact, that day over lunch I mentioned that very thing to Jim. I told him that I was not in the position to even buy a little pop-up camper much less a motorhome. Being the man of God Jim was, he always had an answer ready for you. His response was, "if God wants you to do this, He will make a way, and if you need a motorhome, He will give you one"!

I was happy and very content with my life at this point, but I was slowly figuring out that I was going to have to do something. One sunny day, I was laying on a raft just relaxing in our pool. Lynette had gone somewhere with her mother that day, and I was home alone. I had a call coming in on my cell phone and without looking at the number, I answered the call. I heard the voice on the other end of the line say, "Hello Tony, this is John Gardner with Amazing Grace Missions; how have you been doing?" John had called to tell me that Jim had several fair events on schedule that were already paid for and under contract. He wanted to know if I might be willing to help them out by stepping in and covering these events. How could this be? I had never done anything like this before in my life, but he indicated they would help get me started, train me, and show me how the program works; they just needed help.

After that phone conversation, I'm laying on my back on that raft just floating around in my pool looking up at the sky. As the clouds were floating by, I began to talk to God. Here I was, just trying to relax, but I felt so exhausted! The questions started flowing out of my mouth: "God, how am I supposed to do this?" "Why me?" "What is the purpose?" With those questions came another, and another, and yet another. I knew at some point I needed to talk to Lynette about this, and I'll be honest, I wasn't looking forward to that conversation. I reminded God of the fact that I had already given almost forty years of my life to the music ministry and family ministry. I also explained that Lynette had served him and had even traveled around the world in the mission fields of India. Here I was, trying to negotiate a deal with God who had been calling me to do more for Him. I thought all the past service I had rendered was enough, and yes, I was trying to justify that by asking God to consider that, but it was obvious that God felt there was more I could do and He had another plan.

It was time for a vacation! I told Lynette that I thought we just needed to get out of town for a few days. She had just finished up another school year with a bunch of little third graders, so she was in on the idea. We quickly packed the car and headed south to Florida for some much-needed time to ourselves. The whole time we were in Florida all the events of recent days back home were on my mind. Once you've been with your spouse as long as Lynette and I have been together, it really doesn't take long for one of you to figure out that there is something going on. One morning while sitting with our feet in the ocean watching the waves roll in and out, Lynette asked me what was on my mind. With that, I knew it was time to open up with her and discuss the feelings I was having, the phone call I received from John Gardner, and most importantly to ask her to pray about all of this stuff.

Immediately Satan showed up on the scene. Like me, Lynette had become very comfortable with where we were in life. She expressed her feelings loud and clear and let me know straight up that she was not going to be going out and working in the fairs and festivals, trying to win souls. It's not that she is not concerned about the souls of those who are heading to hell, but we had been on the road for so long, and she thought we had already done our part. She also informed me that God was calling me, but He had not said a word to her about all of this and our conversation that day was actually the first she was hearing about it from me! I had to just change the subject as there were a lot of questions coming up that I didn't have the answers to. I learned a long time ago that Lynette is a woman who likes to have a plan or at least know how the plan is going to work out. Since I couldn't provide the answers she wanted to hear, I just stopped talking about it.

On the trip home from Florida, Lynette was sitting in the passenger's seat reading a book. I had been driving for several hours, and there had been very little conversation between the two of us. There was no radio on, it was quiet, and even the road noise was very low when Lynette looked over to me and asked me what I was thinking. How did she know I was thinking about anything? I lied to her as I said, "I'm not thinking about anything!" I told her I was just driving along being quiet so she could enjoy her book. She said, "You're lying, what are you thinking about"? At that point of our road trip home, I had counted hundreds of motorhomes that we had passed on the highway. When I told her what I had been doing, her comment was, "Tony, get that off of your mind! Whatever you do, don't go home and get us in debt for a motorhome"! My response for that moment was, "I'm just thinking, if all these people can afford to drive a motorhome around, if God thinks we need a motorhome, He will give us one!" (I felt comfortable in making that statement as that is pretty much what Jim Steed had told me. Jim said, *"If God thinks you need a motorhome, he will provide one."*

Sometimes you just have to know when to shut up. Did I know what was really in the future for the two of us? No! Did I understand that it was going to take a step of faith? Yes! However, I came to the conclusion during this trip that I needed to just stand still and wait upon the Lord. While I continued to pray about things, I gave it all to God, and I was willing to wait for a clear answer. And yes, I expressed my faith to the Lord and told Him that I knew for certain He was going to provide me with everything I needed! This was a huge step of faith for me, and while I was uncertain of what the outcome would be, I was excited to see what God was going to do!

> Exodus 14:13—"And Moses said unto the people, Fear ye not, stand still, and see the salvation of the Lord, which he will shew to you to day."

A Minute of Meditation

Has there ever been a time in your life when you felt God was calling you to service? Can you relate to how quickly Satan stepped in to try to silence that calling? So often, we are driven by the fear of the unknown. It is common to have questions, and I think that is alright. However, it is very important for us to realize that if God is calling us to do a work for him, if He brings us to that work, He is going to help us do that work! Taking a step of faith with Christ should not be a battle. If we will just step out in faith, we will find that God just wants us to experience the blessings He had in mind for us all along! What is it that God is asking you do today? Do you have the faith it takes to get the job done?

Chapter 18

Sometimes You Have to Let Go

Is it a *step* of faith, or is it more like a *leap* of faith? Evangelist T. D. Burgess was a preacher who often came and held revivals for us at Mt. Pleasant Baptist Church. He was always a blessing, and when our boys were little, they would get in the car after the service and tell us that he was their favorite preacher. He had a great sense of humor and a very special way of keeping your attention. I remember a joke he shared one time about a man who was walking in the mountains just enjoying the scenery. He stepped a little too close to the edge of the mountain and started to fall. In desperation, he reached out and grabbed a limb of a gnarly old tree that was hanging there on the side of the cliff. Full of fear, he assessed his situation. He was about 100 feet down from the top of the cliff at this point and around 900 feet from the floor of the canyon below. If he lost his grip on that limb he was hanging onto, he would plummet to his death. Afraid for his life, he cried out, "Help me!" But there was no answer. Again and again, he cried out but to no avail. Finally he yelled, "Is anybody up there?" A deep voice replied and the rest of the conversation went like this; "Yes, I'm up here." "Who is it?" "It's the Lord." "Can you help me?" "Yes, I can help." "Help me!" "Let go." Looking around, the man became full of panic. "What?!?!" "Let go, I will catch you." The man's last words were, "Uh … Is there anybody else up there?"

Much like this man, we simply fail to trust God! Far too often we have little to no confidence in the God-given talents and abilities that are within each of us. Something I think we need to understand is this: God not only calls people to service, but He equips them and prequalifies them for the job He is asking them to do. Why on earth would it be any other way? Satan seems to know what is going on because it's when we take a step or leap of faith that the fiery darts start flying at us. That's why the scripture tells us to put on the whole armor of God. The apostle Paul wrote in Ephesians 6 these words; "Finally, my brethren, be strong in the Lord, and in the power of his might. *Put on the whole armor of God,* that ye may be able to stand against the wiles of the devil." It's when those fiery darts of the devil are flying at you and past you that you realize just how important the "whole armor of God" really is.

I had to make a decision about what I was going to do about the fairs that John Gardner had called me about. How would I respond? Still unsure about what I should do, my cell phone rang and it was a pastor of a Baptist Church who was calling to talk to me about what he heard had happened to Jim Steed and how God was going to use me to step in and take over for Jim in the fair ministry. This was a total surprise to me, and it really caught me off guard. This pastor and his congregation supported Jim and the fair ministry he had been involved in for several years. Aware of Jim's passing, and aware of the fact that I was with Jim when he died, this pastor asked if I would care to come to his church and just share my testimony about how things happened and how I was going to step in and fill the gap with this ministry. While it was not funny at all, I couldn't help but laugh as I asked him where he heard this. He goes on to tell me that Jim's wife told him that she thought I was going to step in and take over where Jim left off. While I agreed to go and share my testimony with his congregation, I explained over the phone that day that it seemed God had told everyone but me what was going on and I remember saying, "I sure wish He would tell me."

Lynette was unable to go with me the day I was scheduled to speak at this pastor's church. Our youngest son Parker had to report back to college in Morgantown that day so they loaded up and headed north, and I got in my car and headed south. I had a few hours that morning on the drive to the church to get my thoughts together. Honestly, when I got up to share my testimony with those folks, I had thought about what I was going to say and thought I knew. When you give things to God and ask Him to help you say the things He wants you to say, it will amaze you how His Spirit will come on the scene. It was a total shock at how God moved in the service that day!

I basically shared with these folks who had faithfully supported Jim in the fair ministry over the years the story of how things had unfolded right before my eyes over the past month or so. I told the story of the lunch Jim and I shared a few weeks before his death, right up to where God had me right there on the church property where Jim was the day he died and how the Lord used our pastor's wife and myself to do CPR on Jim until the paramedics arrived. I thanked their pastor for calling me and asking me to come and share what happened and to tell how I was going to step in and take over where Jim left off with the fair ministry. I remember saying, "I wish I could tell you that I'm going to do this, but I just don't know how I'm ever going to be able to do it unless God makes a way." Without a doubt, I said exactly what God wanted me to say. I shared my heartfelt story of how God had used Jim to encourage me to get busy winning people for the Lord. I also shared how I really didn't know how I was going to do it, but I knew if I was supposed to step in and keep this work going that God would give me clarity in the matter and would certainly make a way for me to do it.

After speaking and sharing my testimony, I took my seat down in front of the church with the rest of the congregation as the pastor was preparing to give the message. Several of the folks came up to me and thanked me for sharing, and every one of them had great things to say about Jim and the fair ministry. It was a blessing to hear these folks sharing stories with me of how God used Jim to reach some of their family members and friends for the Lord. Not only was it a blessing, but I was very encouraged by the comments each person was giving me. It was that day that I realized God had a plan, and it really did include me! Like the guy in the story I shared in the opening paragraph of this chapter, I was holding on to a gnarly limb, afraid to let go and let God take care of things. Once I did let go, He had my full attention as He caught me and sat my feet on the ground so I could get busy doing the work He had been asking me to do.

The choir began to sing as the regular preaching service was about to begin. The folks that came up to shake my hand and give me words of encouragement were making their way back to their seats in the congregation when I felt a tap on my shoulder. I turned, and the last gentleman who had shaken my hand came back up and bent down and asked if he could sit down beside of me there for a minute. I slid down the pew to make room, and this gentleman sat down and leaned over to ask if I he and his wife could take me to lunch after the service. I explained that I would need to eat something and that I would be honored to go to lunch with the two of them.

Over the years that our family traveled and ministered, someone asking to take you to lunch was a very common practice. While I had never met this couple before, I had gone to lunch or dinner many times before with folks I didn't know, so this was not uncommon. Once the service was over, I thanked the pastor for the invitation to come and share my testimony and told him

I hope it encouraged someone to get busy winning souls; then it was off to lunch!

Lunch was excellent, and it was a real blessing hearing these folks share stories with me of how they worked with Jim on several occasions winning souls in the fairs. Once again I was reminded of how many times Jim had asked me to come out and just see what it was all about, but my heart was saddened as I realized from listening to these folks that I had missed out on some great blessings by never taking Jim up on the invitation. Unaware of how God had moved in the hearts of these folks during the service, before we left the restaurant, they told me they wanted to assist in helping with the purchase of that motorhome I mentioned in my testimony. Immediately, some of the last words Jim told me over lunch just a few days before he passed were brought to my attention: *"Tony, God knows your needs. If He wants you to do this ministry, He will make a way for you to do this ministry! If you need a motorhome, God is able to give you a motorhome!"*

What an amazing day it had been! On my way back home, I called Lynette to see how her day had gone and to make sure she had made it to Morgantown with Parker. We were sharing how both of our days had been, and she asked me how the church service went. I explained that God moved and I had just finished lunch with a wonderful couple who certainly have a heart for work of the Lord. I guess she could sense a different tone in my voice, and she asked why these folks wanted to take me to lunch. When I told her the reason, I think she thought I was losing my mind or something. In disbelief, she just said, "We will have to talk about this when you get home."

For the next couple of hours as I'm driving home, Satan was riding right along with me in my car. Without a doubt, God was working out all the details, and things were lining up for me to actually step up and help out with the fairs that John Gardner had contacted me about. How could I deny that God was not asking me to do this? I had given Jim every excuse known to man as to why I couldn't do what he did, but how was I going to give God an excuse when the events of this day had played out the way they did? Satan was doing a pretty good job of planting thoughts of doubt in my head as I was driving along. Satan kept saying this "was not going to happen, this couple will not do what they said they would like to do." He also reminded me that I had to convince Lynette that this is what God is asking us to do. The devil already had me believing before I even shared the whole story with Lynette that she was not going to be in agreement with this idea.

I visualized myself hanging on to that gnarly tree limb as my entire body dangled above a rocky canyon floor that was nine-hundred feet below. Was I going to keep making excuses or was I going to trust God and let go? The amazing people I just met gave me their word that they wanted to help and a plan of action was discussed and put into place over lunch. The ball was now in my court, I either had to trust God and have faith that this is exactly what He wanted me to do, or I was going to allow Satan to keep my voice silent and miss out on the blessings that God was wanting me to have. What was I going to do?

> Proverbs 3:5–6—"Trust in the LORD with all thine heart; and lean not unto thine own understanding. In all thy ways acknowledge him, and he shall direct thy paths."

A Minute of Meditation

I hate to think about the blessings I have missed out on throughout my life simply because I wouldn't let go and let God take care of all the details and concerns I carried around with me.

Rather than trusting God, I allowed Satan to convince me that I couldn't do the things God often asked me to do. Have you every experience this in your life? Can you think of a battle you lost and blessings you missed out on because of your lack of faith? I would like to encourage you by reminding you that if you are a child of God, you have access to His riches. If He wants you to have it, you will have it. Don't ever doubt Him. Just let go!

Chapter 19

The Evidence of Things Not Seen

There have been countless times in my life and I'm sure in yours when God was working behind the scenes on things that we were not even aware of. We could save ourselves a lot of worry if we would just understand that He has things in control. I'll admit, sometimes it's hard to understand or even accept what is taking place in our lives, but the fact is God has a plan and a purpose for everything. If we would just learn to trust Him for everything, life in general would be much simpler.

Anytime I've ever felt that God was asking me to do anything, I always knew what was about to take place. If you claim to be a child of God, it's no different for you. It's like all the demons of hell are called to attention by Satan himself and put in attack mode. I sincerely believe that Satan is aware of those God is calling. It seems the minute we start doing whatever it is that God is asking us to do, Satan thinks he can stop God's plan of action for our lives. Maybe it's because he has had a lot of success in defeating those who are doing a work for God that he works so hard. Regardless of why, it's when you start doing things that matter to God that Satan becomes very interested in you and wants to put a stop to you moving forward with God's plan for your life!

I mentioned some verses found in Ephesians 6 in the last chapter and referenced "putting on the whole armour of God" that is found in verse 11. From that verse down to verse 17 the whole armor of God is described to us. If you read this passage of scripture, it's important for us to take note of the next three verses, (vv. 18–20). These verses give us instructions for the battle that is to come. You see, making sure you have all the components that are described as the whole armor of God is very important. However, what is more important is that we understand we are just being prepared for the battle that is certain to come.

I remember my dad and his brothers telling stories about their time spent overseas during World War II. They made it very clear that when you're in the heat of the battle, that is when you are the closest to God! Dad said he knew several men who met God face-to-face in a fox hole, and it was not uncommon for those who were pinned down under fire to call on God. While the type of battle my dad and uncles described is different from a spiritual warfare, it's important to understand what we need to do when we find ourselves in that position. You will notice in the verses that follow those that are telling us to put on the whole armor of God that we are instructed to "boldly pray in the Spirit." Why do you think that is important? Well, in my opinion, it shows me that God is very much aware of the fact that Satan is going to come after you, but even more so once you start doing an eternal work that involves God's kingdom to come!

When we pray in the Spirit, please understand, it means we are praying with the utmost respect and belief that the God we are praying to is going to hear and answer our prayers. I'm not talking about praying in what some believe is an "unknown tongue"; we are simply praying and placing our total faith in the God who promises to deliver when we don't doubt him. During this time in my life, I was really struggling with so many things and knowing that it was God speaking to my heart and asking me to step out and do this thing that was placed right in front of me to do, was just one of those things.

Have you ever found yourself praying about a certain situation, but then when things line up exactly the way you've been praying, you find yourself standing there in unbelief? How can that be? First off, we should never allow that to happen, but it does happen. In a lot of ways, I think it's all a part of the battle. Those thoughts of unbelief come directly from Satan, and we all know this to be true. However, if we would quit questioning God and just follow Him, we would see the blessings He has in mind for us a whole lot sooner! Maybe we would experience more joy for our journey as well.

There are so many stories that we read about in God's Word where people like you and me who were blessed to walk along with Jesus here on this earth when he was here. They witnessed firsthand the many miracles he performed. For them, before the miracle, just like us, they were only seeing the dark side of things. What they failed to realize was, Jesus was fully aware of their situation and had things totally in control. Nevertheless, the miracles took place, they witnessed them, they lived through them, and because of the miracle-working power they experienced, they couldn't help but to tell others of what God had done! Like those people, many of us have had miracles take place in our life, but we fail to share God's goodness or even acknowledge that it is because of God that these amazing things have happened for us.

If we fail to give God the glory, my friends, we are guilty of allowing Satan to silence our voice of victory! Have I experienced modern-day miracles in my life? Yes, many times! Was I always faithful to give God the glory? No! At this particular time in my life, in the middle of a spiritual battle between good and evil, I was boldly praying. While praying, I was seeking answers from God about very specific directions that I needed, and God answered those prayers. I'll never forget the day I drove that motorhome off the lot in Kentucky and was headed for home. The overwhelming feeling as I was driving was a very special visit from God that day. Lynette was following along behind me in our car, and there I was, just me, God, and the open road. I was living and witnessing direct answers to prayers as God sent the answers needed for me to know that I had to step out and do exactly what He had been calling me to do at that given moment.

Over the next six years of my life, I watched as God gave me so many wonderful blessings. I met and talked to literally thousands of people from all walks of life sharing the story of Jesus. Some were not at all receptive to anything I had to say; however, there were thousands who sat down with me and allowed me to share the plan of salvation with them. Not only did I get to share the plan of salvation, but I was blessed to be able to pray with these folks and lead them in the sinner's prayer as they decided to follow Jesus!

There are so many stories I could share of how God used me to help others in their time of need. God never failed to amaze me as I was out working in fairs and festivals. My eyes were opened to the fact that, as John 4:35 says, "the fields are white and ready to harvest"! I've often wondered about how many blessings I missed out on because I never took Jim Steed up on his invitation to go out with him just to see what it was all about. For the longest time, it really bothered me how things happened in order to get my attention about witnessing and doing what I could to win the souls of men, women, boys, and girls of all ages for Christ. I just had to accept that everything happens for a reason and that it's all in God's wonderful plan.

The evidence of things not seen is so much more than anything I could ever describe to you in a book. In my case, the motorhome was just one of many things that came to pass in light of the way I was praying. God ultimately provided the finances, the health and strength, and even the confidence I needed to do the job He was asking me to do. While living through this, I was reminded often of the provisions God was sending to see this work continue. In closing out this particular chapter, I want to share this very special story with you in the hope that it will cause you to see your potential when you simply allow God to have full control of your life.

It was a very warm summer evening in August, and I had been out in the heat pretty much all day, reaching out to folks at a state fair. Things had been pretty slow as the crowd was down that day, and it was one of those times when Satan was talking loud and clear in my ear. I was there alone, the heat had been very intense all day, while I had eaten off and on throughout the day, and my stomach was telling me I was hungry, but something else was telling me I just needed to stay where I was. The sweat was dripping off the end of my nose and running down my back, and all the while Satan was telling me, "It's just not worth it"! Suddenly my eyes made contact with two young Asian girls who were standing across from where I was set up. It was a scene I'll never forget. Both of them had stuffed animals wrapped around their necks that they had won and were just standing there watching one of the carnival rides, trying to decide if they were brave enough to get on it for another thrill. Something said, "Walk over there and start up a conversation," so I did.

These two young ladies had only been in the United States for two weeks. They came here from China to attend medical school and was just out for the evening, enjoying all the events of the fair. I told them that I couldn't help but notice their smiles and asked if I could give them one of the "Smile Jesus Loves You" tracts that I always handed out. Both girls gladly took one of the little booklets, and I told them to enjoy the rest of their evening. I turned and walked back over to our tent and noticed these young ladies had opened the little books and was standing there reading them. Softly, I whispered a pray and asked God to use that book to speak to their hearts, and the next thing I knew, they came walking straight toward me.

"Excuse me, sir; could we ask you some questions"? They wanted to know who Jesus was. Imagine talking to someone who had never heard about Jesus. These girls were well-educated individuals who knew absolutely nothing about Jesus and never knew there was a book called the Bible that told of Him and shared about His life. Needless to say, they were very interested, and I was thrilled to have the opportunity to be the one who was sharing this information with them, apparently, for the very first time in their lifetime.

For the next hour, I shared the scriptures with these young ladies. While reading verses throughout the Bible to them, I could see God moving and working there in front of me that evening. After showing them what the Bible says we have to do to inherit eternal life, both of these girls asked me if I could teach them to pray. Together, we bowed our heads, and I was blessed to lead them in the sinner's prayer. After we prayed, both girls had tears running down their cheeks and dripping off their chins. Before they left, they asked if they could take pictures of the various scriptures I had shared with them so they could send them in a message to China to share with their families as they wanted them to know this amazing story!

What a reminder it was to me that night of the importance of listening to the voice of God. Had I not taken that leap of faith, I would have never experienced that unseen blessing I really never saw coming. I can only hope that somehow those scriptures these young ladies took pictures of were able to reach the hearts of their family members in China. There's one thing I'm certain of: God's Word is going to accomplish everything it is supposed to accomplish; but it takes someone sharing it for others to see and understand its value! Don't live below the blessings God wants you to have in this life. Be faithful in the little things He is asking you to do, as it might just be the reason someone misses hell.

> Isaiah 55:11—"So shall my word be that goeth forth out of my mouth: it shall not return unto me void, but it shall accomplish that which I please, and it shall prosper in the thing whereto I sent it."

A Minute of Meditation

Perhaps there have been times in your life when you questioned God as fear swelled up inside of you. You were really not sure how you were supposed to react, or even what your next step would be, but there was something that kept calling you to action. Satan's voice seemed to be a voice you could hear loud and clear, but you found it hard to hear and understand exactly what it is that God was asking you to do. I would ask you, do you really understand what *faith* is? If you want a life that is full of unexpected blessings, let me encourage you to live and walk by faith! Don't allow Satan to silence you; trust God and listen for His voice. You will be amazed with the outcome!

Chapter 20

Missing My Mother's Prayers

A mother is the glue that holds a family together! I never had to wonder if my mother loved me because she told me she loved me all the time. I was the baby of the family and the only boy, and I'll be the first to admit, I was a momma's boy! Having two sons of my own, I understand why boys tend to cling to their mothers. Now that I have three granddaughters, I totally understand why little girls are daddy's girls! The boys know they can squeeze some extra special attention from their mothers and those little girls know how to squeeze the hearts of their daddy to get exactly what they want as well.

My two older sisters married young and moved out to start a family life of their own, leaving me at home as the only child. I missed having them around the house; however, I soon learned that I had the undivided attention of my parents. Mom lost two sisters at a very young age, and she ended up being raised as an only child. She talked about that a lot, and it was obvious that she understood the loneliness a child can go through with no other siblings in the house. Because of that, my mother always made it a point to make time to do special things with me.

After Dad passed away in 1978, for several years, it was just me and Mom. Things were certainly different, and like any young kid who has lost a parent at a young age, I began to experience a lot of daily struggles in life. Mom recognized this, and as much as I was struggling, she had her own set of problems as she was trying to adjust to life without my dad there as well. I loved spending time with Dad hunting and fishing, working out in the garden, or going out with him as he worked various jobs; and not having him in my life created a major void. There's nothing that can take the place of your dad or your mother no matter what you try to put in the hollow spot that is left in your heart once they are gone!

The day came when my mother decided it was time to sit me down and have a serious talk. I was in the middle of my teenage years, and if you've lived through those years, you know how easy it is to get distracted. Mom was trying to set the record straight with me early on. I'll never forget the conversation as she said, "Tony, I've never had to be a dad and a mother at the same time. I want to give you some freedom, but I want you to know how it's going to work. I'm going to let you start making some decisions for yourself. However, if I feel like there needs to be some adjustments made with your decision, I'll be the one who will make those adjustments. Don't disappoint me!" Were there times I did things I knew she would not approve of? Haven't we all done things that our parents would not approve of? Of course, we have! But I will say, I was never presented with an opportunity to do anything I knew I shouldn't be doing without first thinking how that act would disappoint my mother if she ever found out about it. I know for certain the conversation she had with me kept me from doing a lot of things I could have done.

Mom knew how music was my way of escape. Thank God, she liked music as well because I would have driven her crazy had she not. Pretty much every spare minute I had, I would be in my bedroom playing my bass guitar along with gospel albums that I had collected over the years. Growing up in a home that had a love for gospel music bled right down upon me, and it became a very important part of my life then and going forward. Some kids have dreams of becoming a doctor, a lawyer, a police officer, or a professional athlete; my dream was to become a professional musician. While spending all that time alone in my bedroom, playing with all the professional groups of that day and time, I was working on perfecting my talent and dreaming of one day having the opportunity to climb on a tour bus and hit the road. God blessed me as I eventually got that opportunity, and throughout a major part of my life, I climbed on a lot of different buses and was blessed to travel to a lot of places playing music and using my talent for the Lord.

I had the full support of my mother all those years. I'm sure she may have worried about me being gone so much, but at the same time she knew that I was serving God somewhere in a church or at a gospel concert. For me, it just became the new normal way of life. Most of the time, the bus would pull up across from the house, and before I would walk out of the house to leave for the next trip, Mom would say, "I'll be praying for you!" Had Dad still been living, I'm not sure he would have been as open to the idea of me traveling all over the country and being away from home as much as I was. I've often thought about that, and again, I know it all had to be a part of God's plan for my life.

Even after Lynette and I bought our first home and got married, I always knew that my mother was praying for me. Mom was still living when I started doing the fair ministry. While traveling in the family ministry, for several years prior to stepping out and doing the fair work, I had a lot of experience driving our bus. My father-in-law basically took care of all the maintenance on the bus as well as all of the scheduling for our family ministry, and he started turning more and more of the driving over to me and Lynette's brother. Looking back at that, I could see that I was being prepared for the time when I would be stepping out to do what we did. God had given us a new motorhome, and Mom was aware of the fact that now it would be me and

Lynette traveling alone out on the road without the rest of the family. Not that she didn't have confidence in my ability to drive the motorhome, but she had a whole new set of concerns and worries, I guess, as a mother. Even then, I never had to wonder if Mom was praying for me because she was always faithful to tell me she would be praying.

I tried to call Mom pretty much every night, especially when we were out traveling and away from home. She always wanted to know how many people gave their life to Christ on any given night, and before our call would end, she would say; "I'll be praying for you tomorrow and look forward to hearing what God does as you reach out to others!" I drew strength from those conversations as I knew I could always count on my mother's prayers. She was my biggest fan, supporter, encourager, and could build my confidence up better than anyone!

My world was rocked on January 9, 2014, as God decided that Mom had suffered long enough. She had been battling cancer for a long time, and while none of us wanted to see her go, we all knew her quality of life here was over. God had a better plan for her, and I wouldn't bring her back here if I could. I knew she was going to a much better place, she would be reunited with my dad who had been gone for years, she would see her dad and mother and even her two little sisters that she lost many, many years ago. However, while I was faced with saying another good-bye down here, Satan was already hard at work in my mind, and another battle was on!

Suddenly, I was faced with a whole new way of life. Life for the first time without my mother. Life for the first time without my mother's prayers. How could I go on without her? All I could think about was how different life in general was going to be. In times like these, Satan works overtime on us, and for me, he was pouring it on! I guess I thought Mom would just always be there for me, but the fact that she was gone was weighing extremely heavy on my heart. Somehow, I had to pick up the broken pieces and move on. I just didn't know how I was going to do it.

> Deuteronomy 4:9—"Only take heed to thyself, and keep thy soul diligently, lest thou forget the things which thine eyes have seen, and lest they depart from thy heart all the days of thy life: but teach them to thy sons and thy sons' sons."

A Minute of Meditation

One of the greatest things we can do for our children is to pray for them! Knowing that my mother was praying for me gave me peace that is hard to describe. After her passing, I was troubled inside because I knew I would never hear her say that she would be praying for me ever again. Satan used that thought so many times on me in an effort to discourage me and to make me think that I couldn't go on without her prayers. I discovered that I had to pick up where my mother left off. It was now my responsibility to make certain that I was praying for myself. More importantly, I needed to make sure I was praying for my own children and grandchildren, never forgetting the things I was taught and learned from my mother. I would like to encourage you to carry the torch for your family. Pray for them daily. Most importantly, teach them to pray! You will never regret it!

Chapter 21

A New Way of Life

I was fifty years old when Mom passed away, and I suddenly found myself feeling like a scared little boy all over again. I had experienced life for a number of years without Dad, but I had never known a world or lived life ever before without both of my parents. My world had been shaken to the core this time, and I really wasn't sure how I would be able to keep on going without having Mom as my go-to person. I could always count on her to have all the answers to my problems, and even though I was a grown man, there were still times I would depend on my mother for direction.

A year or so prior to Mom's passing, our oldest son Zach and his wife Kayla had mentioned that they were thinking about trying to adopt a child. We were so excited for them as things started moving forward with their thought process. It became a matter of prayer for our entire family, and Mom was right in the middle of all those prayers. She was excited about the idea, and I know for certain that she prayed about this every day once we told her about Zach and Kayla's decision to adopt.

Throughout the last year of Mom's time with us, there had been several possibilities for adoption that came up. The process was like a roller coaster ride with a lot of ups and downs, twists and turns, and more often than not, there were some major drop offs where things ended up in a crash-and-burn situation. After several failed attempts, Zach and Kayla decided to get involved in the foster system as they wanted to help kids and was also searching for an opportunity to give a child a forever home if possible.

After looking into the adoption process, we soon found out that this could be a very costly process. Thanksgiving was always one of Mom's favorite times of the year, and it was a time we all set aside to be together as a family. The last Thanksgiving we got to spend with Mom was in November of 2013. After our family dinner that year, Mom had something she wanted to say to the whole family. We all knew her health was failing her, so we sat up at attention, listening to what she had to say. Mom said, "I've got a request of all of you this year. I know I'm not going to be here much longer, and I don't need a thing. Just having us all together means everything to me and that's enough. Rather than you guys buying me gifts for Christmas, I want to ask that you just give me money instead." That was pretty much all she had to say, so we all went back to eating our deserts and trying to enjoy the rest of the day together.

Christmas 2013 rolled around the next month, and once again we all found ourselves gathered together at Mom's house to celebrate her other special time of the year with her. Our family can never get together without eating, so again, there was a nice meal involved. After dinner, it was time to pass out the gifts to the kids, and it was also time for us to give Mom what she asked for. Everyone did exactly what she asked us to do and that was to give her money. She opened her card and pulled out all the money and said she had something she wanted to say. Mom reminded all of us of the fact that she was not going to be with us much longer. I believe she knew that for sure. She then started talking about how she had been praying for Zachary and Kayla, and she said she knew she would probably not be here to meet the child that God had in mind for the two of them.

However, she wanted to give the money everyone had given her to Zach and Kayla and wanted them to use it for their adoption or to buy something that was needed for their baby once God gave them one.

Just a few days after this, Mom left us for her eternal home in heaven. Knowing how she felt and after hearing everything she had to say, this made things even more difficult for me now that she was gone. Satan jumped up on my shoulder once again and began to speak discouraging words in both my ears. I was finding it hard to understand why Mom couldn't be here with us to see the gift we were anticipating would come to Zach and Kayla. Why did God have to take her from us? Bitterness began to build up in my heart, as I had feelings I had never experience ever before.

There are a lot of things that I hold within and just don't share with anyone. Sometimes, I just don't feel like those around me really understand how I feel. I lost the special bond there was between me and my mother. I had those frightened feelings I got as a young boy after losing Dad, and as a grown man, here I was again questioning God and not understanding why things had to be the way they were at that moment. I know God understands those feelings I had, and in the midst of my grief, I also knew He was ready to teach me a lesson. It was time for me to adjust to *a new way of life!*

John 14:18—"I will not leave you comfortless: I will come to you."

A Minute of Meditation

Has there ever been a time in your life when you felt like the rug was pulled out from under you? It seems when we finally get to a point in life where we have a good handle on things, suddenly life changes. We go from being comfortable to being overwhelmed. Our emotions change like the wind. We have those moments when we feel like we are on top of the mountain, but then we blink and find ourselves in the bottom of the lowest valley. Simply put, life changes! I would like to encourage you to trust God when these new challenges show up in your life. Don't allow Satan to silence you and stop you from enjoying the new way of life that God has presented to you. Walk with God and know that He will be with you every step of the way.

Chapter 22

He Giveth and He Taketh Away

January 9, 2014 was a day I wish I never had to live through. My sisters and I had been by the bedside of our mother pretty much all day that day. At that time the nurses from Hospice were coming in daily to check on Mom as her condition had continued to get worse by the hour. We were given an estimated time line of how long they thought Mom would be with us, and while it is only a guess, the folks at Hospice have been around these situations enough that they have a really good feel for these things.

Thinking we still had a few days, I decided to drive home to take a shower, change clothes, and pick up Lynette so she could go back with me to sit with Mom that night. Unfortunately, shortly after I got to my home, the phone rang, and my brother-in-law informed me that Mom was gone. Why? Why would God allow me to come home and not be there with my mother when her crossing time came? I just couldn't believe it. Why? I will forever have that question on my mind, but at the moment, all I could do was accept the fact that obviously God knew best.

Somehow I feel like Mom didn't want me to be there when she left us. She had been struggling with the thoughts of leaving us anyway, but I really think she didn't see me as an adult. To Mom, I was still her baby boy, and I sincerely believe she didn't want me to see her take her last breath. Walking back into her bedroom and seeing her lifeless body lying there in her bed was the worst thing I've ever had to endure, and I'm sure God knew I would not have been able to handle her passing right in front of my very own eyes.

Seeing someone you love suffering is a very hard thing to watch. Knowing things were never going to get any better for Mom had caused us all to accept the fact that we just needed to be thankful for every day we were given with her this side of heaven. After the doctors had given her the diagnosis of having colon cancer with no treatment options available to her due to her age and other various medical conditions she had, Mom refused to give up. She told us all that this was just a bump in the road. She didn't want us to worry as she knew everything was going to be alright.

Once the reality of things set in for me and my sisters, we were determined to make the best of every day we were given to spend with Mom. We asked the doctor before leaving the hospital to take Mom home if there were any restrictions or special directions we needed to follow in relation to taking care of our mother. Her doctor explained that she could do whatever she wanted to do as long as she felt like doing it. Anyone who knew my mother knows she enjoyed taking trips and traveling. One of her granddaughters lived in Tampa, Florida, with three of her great-grandchildren, and she loved visiting Tampa every chance she got. Needless to say, a trip to Tampa was soon scheduled. Mom also loved visiting Pigeon Forge, Tennessee, so a trip to Pigeon Forge was planned. For the next three years, God allowed us to take trips and enjoy this special time with our mother, and she kept going until she got so weak that she just couldn't go anymore.

By the time the first of the year rolled around in 2014, the conversations changed with Mom. It was as if she and God had been talking, and God had told her that she would be making her way into heaven soon. Those conversations were very hard for me, but I'm so glad the Lord allowed us to have them. I would have lunch with her as often as I could, and this gave us opportunities to visit. Every day after work, I would stop by to see her before driving home, and I would always wonder if that was going to be the last time I would get to talk to her here on earth. During those visits, Mom was always assuring me of how much she loved me and she reminded me of the importance of always staying faithful to God.

One of the last quality visits I got to have with Mom will forever be etched in my memory. She felt really good that day and wanted to talk about everything. We both shared memories of the past and talked about how blessed we were as a family, then Mom began talking about the blessings that God had in store for Zachary and Kayla. While she knew in her heart that she wasn't going to be here to see the blessings take place, she wanted us all to keep the faith and know that in God's timing, the blessing was going to come.

I've thought about that conversation a lot since Mom has been gone. January 9, 2014, the Lord took her to heaven, and I found myself in a deep, dark valley for several months. I was trying to keep the faith as we continued to wait on the blessing she kept referring to and assuring us would come. I'll be honest though, there were so many ups and downs and days full of disappointments that came about as a result of all the waiting. The whole process was becoming very discouraging to say the least, and Satan was doing what he does best in causing us to doubt that we would ever experience the blessing Mom mentioned. Eleven months had gone by since Mom was taken from us, and doubt had grown in my heart and mind to the point that I was just about to give up hope that Zach and Kayla would ever get to experience this blessing we had all been praying for. However, in our darkest moments, in December of 2019, our prayers were answered as word came, and we were informed that our blessing was on the way. Once again, the Lord came through!

> Job 1:21—"The Lord gave and the Lord hath taken away; blessed be the name of the Lord."

A Minute of Meditation

As I was writing this chapter, I couldn't help but think about the verse of scripture I shared to finish the chapter out. The story of Job that we read about in the Bible is an amazing testimony of one man's faith and how he stood firm in that faith even through all the trials he faced. I know Job's wife doubted God as she apparently was at her wits end when she told him that he should just curse God and die; but as strong as Job seemed to be through all he faced, I've often wondered if he ever doubted God. However, in the end, it is apparent that his faith held him and kept him strong through it all. Have you ever found yourself feeling like God may be testing you as He did Job? Everything seems to be going just fine in life when suddenly it is like all the forces of hell are let loose against you. The Lord gives and the Lord takes away. In my case at this point in my life, the Lord took something away, but turned right around and gave us another blessing. In your moments of doubt, don't give Satan the pleasure of one single moment of feeling he was victorious in defeating you. Just cry out to the Lord and wait on the blessings to come that He has in store for you!

Chapter 23

Part One of a Double Blessing

I n the final chapter of the book of Job, we read the end of the story, and we see how Job totally submits his life to God. We also see how the Lord blessed him because of his faithfulness. Here is what we are told:

> Then Job answered the Lord, and said, I know that thou canst do everything, and that no thought can be withheld from thee. Who is he that hideth counsel without knowledge? Therefore have I uttered that I understood not; things too wonderful for me, which I knew not. Hear, I beseech thee, and I will speak: I will demand of thee, and declare thou unto me. I have heard of thee by the hearing of the ear; but now mine eye seeth thee: Wherefore I abhor myself, and repent in dust and ashes. (Job 42:1–6)

As I was writing this chapter, I thought about how the story of this man named Job ended. I would encourage you to read the entire book of Job just to get a complete view of everything this man went through. Was he a man of faith? He most certainly was! Did he ever doubt God as he was living through all the loss he experienced? Unlike his wife, who told him he should just curse God and die, it is clear that Job stood firm and never wavered in his faith in God. Unlike this woman who allowed her heart to harden and get bitter because of all the suffering and loss she was seeing thrown upon her husband and their family, Job refused to give up on God and was determined that he would stand strong in his faith, believing that the living God would see him through it all. However, I think these verses of scripture found at the end of the story of Job give us some insight of the fact that Job, like all of us do, probably did doubt God somewhat.

Does doubt cause God to turn His back upon us? Does God hear and answer our prayers, even though we may allow doubt to creep into our lives? My friends, I personally think unconfessed doubt could seriously hinder our prayer life. When we pray and ask God for specific answers, we can't allow doubt to have any place in our hearts and minds. In this story about this man named Job, I believe he developed a new awareness of the wisdom of God's hidden plans for his life. Yes, God gave Satan access to Job, but all the while Satan was throwing all the things he did at Job, it's important for us to understand that God never left Job's side through it all. Not only did Job develop a new awareness of God's wisdom, but I believe he saw the limits of his own wisdom. Through it all, Job realized that he had to rely and depend on God. What I see as the most important thing about his story is the fact that Job had a new sensitivity to his own sin. He admitted that he had a limited perspective, and finally came to the point that he totally submitted to God's will and authority.

On down in verse 12 of the last chapter of the book of Job, we read this: So the Lord blessed the latter end of Job more than his beginning." Job had heard from the voice of God and from a spiritual sense he believed. But once he saw in the physical sense with his own eyes just how blessed his life really was after going through all he had gone through, Job said, "I abhor myself, and repent in dust and ashes." At this point, it's pretty clear that Job did have some doubt as he was disgusted with himself and hated the fact that he allowed the smallest amount of doubt to even have place in his life. He was disappointed and realized that he needed to repent for allowing sin to enter his mind and life.

After losing my mother, I felt like I lost the very best prayer partner I had ever had in my life. I never had to doubt that Mom was praying for me, but after losing the comfort of knowing she was here on earth praying for me, Satan tried to discourage me with those thoughts and caused me to even doubt my own ability to pray for myself. I missed the simple fact that I could pick up the phone and call my mother anytime I wanted. I missed knowing that I could ask her about anything and most of the time be comforted by the fact that she would always have the answers I was looking for. Like Job, it took God getting me to this place where I could see my lack of wisdom before I could clearly see the hidden plans He had in store for my future.

Eleven months after God called my mother home to heaven, in December of 2014, part one of a double blessing arrived. I wish I could tell you that my faith had always been strong, but after all the ups and downs I had seen my oldest son and his wife go through up to this point, I didn't know if I should be excited or not. Lynette and I received a phone call from Zachary, letting us know that he and Kayla were coming home with a little girl. While we were aware of the possibility of this happening, we just didn't allow ourselves to get too wrapped up in the whole process, mainly because of all the prior disappointments we had seen them go through up to this point.

They sent us a picture of her buckled in her little car seat on our phones, and we immediately fell in love! This was real; they were actually on their way home with our first little grand-daughter. The car pulls up and our eyes made contact for the first time with one of the sweetest little girls on earth. The faith we had held onto from a spiritual sense had suddenly became a faith we were physically seeing with our own eyes. God had answered our prayers! Why did I ever doubt Him?

Psalm 37:4—"Delight thyself also in the LORD;
and he shall give thee the desires of thine heart."

A Minute of Meditation

When you pray, do you sincerely take your requests to God and totally believe that He is hearing your prayers and is going to answer them? If so, then you are not doubting Him! I'm sure you are like me, and we are all like Job; there are times when we pray and we doubt, but still God has answered our prayers even though we allowed doubt to enter our hearts and minds. When that happens, God confirms His love for us, and what a blessing it is to know that even when we doubt, He cares enough that He goes ahead and provides the needs and true desires we actually expressed to Him. My friends, don't allow Satan to hinder your prayer life. If anything, once you pray and give things to God, spend any time of doubt that may arise searching your heart, understanding the limits of your own wisdom, admitting your sin of doubt to God, submitting your life to Him, and believing that He has your best interest at heart!

Chapter 24

Part Two of a Double Blessing

A few days had passed, and the second part of our double blessing was about to arrive. Here we were in the early part of December, 2014, with the Christmas season quickly approaching. We had just come through our first Thanksgiving without my mother, and I was dreading this first Christmas without Mom here to spend this special time of the year with us. How in this world could I ever be sad? God had already given us a special gift in our first little granddaughter, Liza Ann, and now He was blessing us with her little sister. Not one granddaughter, but just like that, we were blessed with two!

My thoughts were taken back to the life of Job. The way things were happening, I had to believe that Mom had orchestrated these two special Christmas gifts and sent them to us all the way from heaven! My heart had a hole in it that I never felt would ever be filled again. Up to this point, I had no desire to even think about celebrating Christmas. God knew how I was feeling, and He knew I needed something to get me through this time of the year. So, what did He do? He brought us Part Two of our double blessing.

God brought an end to Job's suffering and eventually set him free to enjoy life again. While I've never gotten over losing my mom, the thought of how everything came about and when it happened caused me to believe that somehow she had asked

God to send these special blessings our way. God's restoration of Job was immediate and bountiful, and when it happened, he was given friends, material prosperity, family, and a happy, long life. My eyes were opened to the fact that God was using all the events of the recent days to restore me as well.

Here I was thanking God for these two special little blessings that came at a vital time in my life. A time that I needed a special touch, I needed to somehow recover from the loss and at least try to enjoy life with the family God had blessed me with. It wouldn't be fair to everyone else if I didn't get back to being some kind of normal. But Satan began to plant additional thoughts of doubt in my mind, trying to rob me of the joy that had been given to me with these two little girls that had suddenly stolen my heart. The thought of being blessed as abundantly as Job had been blessed was just too good to be true. Satan used these thoughts to cause me to doubt that these blessings actually came from God.

December 25, 2014, arrived, the day we celebrate the birth of Jesus, God's son, the greatest gift this world has ever known! I had so many mixed emotions swelling up inside of me. This was the first Christmas ever without my mother, but it was also the first Christmas ever for me with grandkids. Not one, but two! How could I not be happy? When my feet hit the floor that Christmas morning, things were different. I was excited about the schedule of events we had planned for the day. Our boys were married and out of the house, but the thought of seeing happy little faces around our Christmas tree again brought a new hope to me and gave me a new reason for living. No gift could be greater than these two little girls God had brought into our family, but I wanted this to be a very special time for them and was committed to making it as special as it could possibly be.

What a celebration! My heart was full, and once again, I was reminded that we can trust God in all things. Even when doubt may arise, God is still at work, and He still performs miracles in our lives today. He does mend broken hearts! He can fill your life with happiness where sadness may exist. The sparkle that was in Liza's eyes as she opened all her gifts was worth it all to me. As I held little Paisley in my arms, my heart melted from within. When God restores, He does a complete job! When He blesses us, His blessings are always very special. A life in Christ is an abundant life!

Romans 8:28—"And we know that all things work together for good to them that love God, to them who are the called according to his purpose

1 Thessalonians 5:18—"In everything give thanks: for this is the will of God in Christ Jesus concerning you."

A Minute of Meditation

I've discovered throughout my life up to this point, there are certain things that trigger negative thoughts and feelings in our lives. Should we let those thoughts and feelings control us? Absolutely not! It's no surprise, as long as we live here in this world, there are going to be days when we find ourselves walking right down in the middle of a deep, dark valley. Something we should all remember is the fact that when we are down in that valley, we are not walking there alone. Yes, it's true; things happen that discourage us. Those feelings we have when we experience the separation that the death of a loved one brings are very real. Grief, pain, and the heartaches that go along with that separation are all very real. While we hurt down deep inside and while people don't always understand the pain, the hurt, and the emptiness we have; one thing is for sure, God knows what we are going through. In times of loss, Satan will do his best to use those moments to silence us. However, what Satan uses to cause us to feel that we can't possibly get through this moment in time, God uses the same situation to cause us to see the blessings He had in mind for us all along! When you find yourself in a situation like this, remember to *give thanks* because it is all in the will of God concerning you!

Chapter 25

When It Rains, It Pours

My father-in-law often shared this thought when he was preaching, saying, "You can usually find yourself in one of three positions in life, that is, you are in the middle of a storm, you just came out of a storm, or you are getting ready to go into a storm." The older I get, the more I see this to be very true. Just when you think everything is fine, life is good, and things are totally going the way you think they should be, look out!

June 23, 2016, was just another Thursday for me. I was working that day with a client in my office when my cell phone began to ring. I looked down and saw it was my wife and asked my client if it would be okay if I took the call. When I answered the call, immediately I could tell Lynette was upset about something. She asked what I was doing. In disbelief, I asked and responded with, "What do you mean, what am I doing? I'm working!" Lynette quickly said, "You need to wrap things up and get home as quickly as you can!" She was in a total panic.

I proceeded to explain to Lynette that I was in the middle of an account review with my client, and I couldn't just stop what I was doing and leave. Her response was, "If you know what's good for you, you will get in your truck and get home! If you don't leave now, you will not get home!" What was going on? Why was it so important for me to get home? I asked her these questions as she just wasn't making much sense in the conversation. It was then that she explained there was a flash flood warning out for our community, and it was raining like she had never seen it rain before, so in her mind and per the weather emergency alerts that were all over the radio and television, it was going to flood, for sure! I looked out the window of my office, and the sun was shining as brightly as I had ever seen it and not a cloud in the sky. I understood that she was twenty-five miles north of where my office was, but I could not understand how it could be as bad as she was telling it was. There had been no rain in the forecast, and I just couldn't believe it was as bad as she was telling me it was. I told her that I would be home as soon as I got finished up.

Ten minutes passed, and my phone was ringing again. Lynette was calling me back, and I answered again. The conversation went like this; "Have you left yet?" My response, "No!" "Get in your truck and head to the house, now!" I explained that I needed to run by our oldest son's office to pick him up as he rode to work with me that day. Zachary had taken his truck to the shop that morning and needed me to take him to work, this meant that I needed to pick him up and take him home. Lynette just kept saying, "Get home!" I got off the phone and explained what was going on to my client. He was very understanding of the situation and agreed that I should probably get on the road as he had heard the forecast was not looking good for the evening hours. So we wrapped up our meeting, and I headed out.

I called Zach to let him know I was on my way to pick him up. He said he had already received a call from his mother and he would be ready. I drove by his office, and we were on our way. Again, the sun was shining, and it was a beautiful day where we were. We just couldn't believe it was as bad as we were being told it was. Both of us thought this was a total overreaction! That was until we got about nine miles up the road. We finally ran into the rain. This was rain like I had never seen before! You've heard the old expression that it was raining cats and dogs? Well, it was in fact raining cats and dogs! I could not believe what we were seeing. As we drove the next ten miles on I-79 north, there were mud slides coming out on the interstate. Water was shooting off the sides of the mountains out into the lanes of traffic making it almost impossible to drive faster than twenty miles per hour on the interstate. The farther we went, the worse it got! Trees had fallen off the mountain sides and out on the interstate; this was truly unlike anything I had ever seen before in my life.

We made it to our exit only to find that the main route to our home was totally blocked by mud slides with trees across the road and the water from the local stream was coming up into the road as well. We got back on I-79 and headed south back to the next exit, thinking we would go north on Route 119, which would get us around all the mess. It didn't take us long to realize that was not going to happen either. To our disbelief, Route 119 was totally blocked by a little stream that rarely ever got out of its banks. This creek was raging like a mighty river! The water was roaring like some of the best white-water rafting rivers we have in the Mountain State of West Virginia. Needless to say, we were unable to get home, so we decided to drive a few miles back down the road and get us some dinner.

I had seen the Elk River up and out of its banks before, but I had never seen all the destruction I was seeing this time. My thoughts were, this storm will pass, the rain will stop, and the waters will recede. Zach and I went to dinner, thinking the rain would let up, and we would eventually get home, but getting home that evening was not possible. The local motels were full, so we went to Lynette's brother's home and decided it would be best if we spent the night there rather than risking getting stuck out on the road somewhere blocked between the high waters.

Once we got settled in, I called Lynette to let her know where we were. I was glad to hear that she was with her mother, dad, Mom Maw, our daughter-in-law, and two granddaughters, and I assured her that they would all be fine. In a total panic, Lynette begins to tell me that they are all going to die in this flood as the water was continuing to come up and the rain did not seem to be showing any signs of letting up. This conversation was going nowhere, and I was beginning to get very stressed as a result of talking to her. There was absolutely nothing I could do, and I felt totally helpless at that moment.

It was getting very late and while I didn't feel like I would be able to sleep, I did feel that we needed to at least lie down and try to get some sleep if at all possible. I wanted to call Lynette again before I went to bed, and it took several attempts to get her to answer her phone. When I couldn't get an answer, I began to panic myself; finally she answered my call. She explained they had just lost power and were trying to find candles for some light. She gave me an update on the water levels and told me that the water was getting ready to come up on the front porch of her mom and dad's home and again proceeded to tell me that they were going to die. With no power, they didn't have any way to charge their phones, so we agreed it would be best if they turned their phones off to save their batteries. When we said, "I love you" to each other, all I could think about was, "This may be the last time I could ever tell Lynette that I loved her."

I sincerely believe the details of this story will forever be etched in my memory. The next few days were some of the longest days of my life. Phone contact was totally lost as all the cell towers in the area were down. On top of that, with no power, nobody could charge their phones and eventually lost all their battery power, and cell service was totally down. We were unable to get into the community that we lived in for several days. Zach and I were able to get updates on the local news, but the information they were giving out was very limited. There were several fire departments in the area who were now going house to house, doing boat rescue missions, but we still had no news on the whereabouts of our family who had been trapped. The fear of the unknown was really starting to work on my mind, and of course, Satan was at work in my thoughts as I began to think the worse had possibly happened. Not knowing if those you love are dead or alive and having no way of communicating with them makes you pretty sick at your stomach!

A few days had passed and I finally got a phone call on my cell phone from Lynette. The men from the fire department had rescued her, our daughter-in-law Kayla, and our two little grand-daughters, and she was able to get her phone charged to call me. It was a relief to hear her voice and to get the update; however, her mother, dad, and Mom Maw had elected to stay back at the house. That was hard to understand at first, but according to Lynette, they would have never been able to get into the boat due to their age and their physical conditions. And if that didn't get them, trying to get into the truck the National Guard was using to transport people out to safety would have.

We were eventually able to get back into town, and I got my father-in-law, mother-in-law, and my wife's mom maw Betty out of the house and to safety. Our community looked like a war zone. I could not believe my eyes, but it became really clear why Lynette had been in such a panic when I walked into her mom and dad's house. The flood waters had turned things upside down, mud was all throughout the house, but, thank God, everyone survived!

Once everybody was accounted for and was safe and sound, I decided it was time to try to get to mine and Lynette's home as we had pets inside the house that had not eaten in several days. I wasn't sure if they were dead or alive, but I felt it would be best if I went to the house alone so Lynette would not have to face it if something had happened to them. When I opened the door, water started running out of the house. I walked in, and it was totally silent. The feeling I got was very creepy, and I was overcome with one of the worst feelings I have ever experienced in my life. A lot of what we had worked for our entire married life was destroyed! How would we ever recover from this? My main mission at that moment was to check on our pets, and while I was calling out their names, I wasn't hearing anything, so I was thinking the worst had happened.

Our dogs, Baxter and Percy were upstairs when I found them. Both of them were trembling and were a nervous wreck. I was thrilled to find them alive, but I could tell they were in a state of shock. Lynette had just gotten a new little kitten a few weeks before named Chloe, and I could not find her anywhere. I was calling for her and looking everywhere for her as I thought she probably had run under one of the beds or was just hiding some-where; but unfortunately she didn't make it. Chloe somehow got caught in our half bath downstairs and drowned in the flood waters. Needless to say, this was not a very good moment for me.

What a devastating event this was. Not only for our family, but our entire community has suffered now for several years, trying to get everything restored and back to some kind of normal. Lynette and I lost everything in the downstairs of our home, two cars, and everything in our attached garage and a detached garage, along with a motorhome that we used in a min-istry we had been doing. Our son Zachary, his wife Kayla, and their two girls lost everything but his truck that was in the shop. They lost their home and everything in it, plus Kayla's vehicle. Their family basically had the clothes on their backs and that was it. Lynette's dad and mom lost two vehicles and everything in the downstairs and the basement of their home as well as everything in their attached garage and Mom Maw Betty lost her car, her home, a secondary rental dwelling, and everything she owned except the clothes that were on her back.

We all discovered through this terrible event just how much God really loved us. I would not be telling you the truth if I said

I didn't have a lot of concerns and worry during all of this. I'm so very thankful that we still had each other as well as God on our side. In addition, we had so many of our family members, our friends, and even people we had never met before who came to our rescue. What Satan used to try to destroy us, God used for our good! This event brought me to my knees on so many occasions, and He showed me just how little I really need in this life. The lessons I learned about placing my complete trust in God were so valuable to me, not only for the immediate moment, but for the rest of my life. Yes, we suffered great loss, but so did everyone else in our community. I can testify though that the mercy and goodness of God are two wonderful things: His blessings are abundant and He is faithful.

> Matthew 7:25—"And the rain descended, and the floods came, and the winds blew and beat upon that house; and it fell not: for it was founded upon a rock."

A Minute of Meditation

Can you think of a time in your life when the storms came up suddenly and caught you off guard? Maybe something happened that you never dreamed would ever happen to you and your family. Things were totally out of your control, and you were brought to your knees and made to understand just how much your life depends on God. Is your life built upon "The Rock" or have you built on life's shifting sand? My friends, Jesus, the Son of God, is the answer to every storm you and I will ever face. There are so many stories found in the scriptures that involve storms. A great part of the life of Christ was spent around the water. Many of his disciples were fishermen, and they, too, spent a lot of time around the water. They understood that storms would often come up on the seas as they were out in their boats fishing. They also learned firsthand who the Master of seas really was when Jesus came walking toward them on the water. The waves that were rolling over their heads and over their boat were under the feet of Christ as He showed them His power. The storms that tossed them to and fro were made calm at the sound of His voice, and my friends, there is not a storm that you and I will ever face that God is not fully aware of what the outcome will be for us. I challenge you today, to trust Him! Build your house upon "The Rock," that is Jesus Christ! You won't be disappointed!

Chapter 26

After the Storm Passes By

In every situation you find yourself in, you usually don't have to look very far to find someone who is having it a lot worse than you are. After the rain stopped and the waters receded, it was then that you could see all the destruction and devastation around our community. Power in the area had been knocked out, there was no cable service, and our cell service was very limited to say the least. We had pretty much all moved into Lynette's brother's home and our son Zachary, his wife, and children were staying with Kayla's sister and brother-in-law; so we just had to be thankful that we had family close by that had not suffered any damage to their homes, as it provided us with a place to shower, sleep, and eat after spending long days on the cleanup duty that was necessary.

The local news was on top of the situations that were going on around our state. In addition to our community and the surrounding area, there were other areas of our state that was hit just as hard. We heard reports on the radio, and when the cable finally came back on, we were able to watch things unfolding daily on the local news. Reports were pouring in of folks who had lost their lives in this massive flood, and once again, we were all reminded of how blessed we were to still have all of our family, even though we were all going to have to deal with a lot going forward.

While dealing with your own problems can be stressful, being that I am in the insurance business and the fact that I wrote all the insurance for my family members as well as a lot of people in and around our community, who suffered damage, the aftermath of this storm was pounding me with stress. So many claims had to be filed, meetings with adjusters had to be scheduled, dealing with FEMA representatives, local and state government agencies, and on and on it went. Had it not been for all the support staff I had helping me at my office—and God—I would have never gotten through all this!

The words that my father-in-law had shared over the years of our travels when he would preach about, "Us being in the middle of a storm, just coming out of a storm, or getting ready to go into another storm" was sure ringing true in my mind, day and night for the next several months.

There were nights when I would lay my head on my pillow and fall asleep, and have nightmares, reminding me of where I was and what I had to do going forward. Then there were days when I had mud from the bottom of my feet all over me and all the way to the top of my head that I felt like I was living in the worst dream of my life. I could not get my mind wrapped around how we would ever get ourselves restored to at least where we were before the flood or even close to where we were. Lynette and I both cried and prayed a lot. The hardest part for me was when she would ask me questions that I just didn't have the answers to. I tried to remain positive and strong for her, but if I'm honest about everything, I was falling apart!

Knowing that I needed to be the strong one in our situation, I could feel the stress of everything just taking over in my life. Satan was fighting me and bringing everything he had to the battle every day. Stress, my friends, will kill you if you let it, and it about got the best of me. I was a total wreck mentally, physically, and spiritually as I struggled with all the problems and decisions we were faced with as a result of what had happened.

I wrote about losing my dad at a very young age in an earlier chapter; and this was certainly one of those times in my life when I wished he was here to talk to. It was so hard to find anybody to talk to during this time, and with all of our family going through the same thing, I didn't feel like I could open up to anyone. However, when God gave me the father-in-law he gave me; after I became a part of his family, it was like I was his own son. Jack had an amazing way about him and a sense of always knowing when something was bothering me. While we were walking along in the middle of the very same situation, he had such a calm and a peace about him that helped me get through every day. We prayed together so many times and shared our deepest thoughts and concerns with each other; but most importantly, Jack continually reminded me of the necessity of placing it all on God and trusting Him for the best possible outcome.

With each passing day, more and more people were stepping up and coming to our rescue. I wish I had a list of names to share in this book of all the people who helped us after this storm. I don't want to start naming them because I would forget somebody, and I don't want to do that. There are people who came to help us in the cleanup process we didn't even know; so there's really no way of naming everyone. All I know is this: they were all angels sent from heaven! If you are reading this book and you helped in any way with our recovery, you know who you are, but I personally want to say thank you to each and every person who came to our rescue. You're all very special to us, and I know you made God smile when you stepped up and did everything you did for our family and so many more here in our community. We simply don't have the words to adequately thank you, but we will never forget you!

Thomas Mosie Lister was a Baptist minister, singer, and a song writer who wrote some of the greatest Gospel songs ever written in my opinion. One song of his that I dearly love is titled, "Till the Storm Passes By." The words to the chorus of that song says: "Till the storm passes over, till the thunder sounds no more, till the clouds roll forever from the sky; Hold me fast, let me stand, in the hollow of Thy hand; Keep me safe till the storm passes by." God brought us through this horrible storm in our life! Not only did He bring us through it, but He restored us and gave us more than we originally had to begin with. Was it a difficult thing to go through? It most certainly was, but we grew in our faith, and we learned through it all to trust Him more.

If there is one thing I could recommend to you my friends, it would be Jesus. I know for certain that I could never make it one day without Him in my life. He's the greatest thing that has ever happened to me. Will there be storms in your life? For sure, you will face the storms of this life. Remember, you are in one of three places: in the middle of a storm, just coming out of a storm, or you're getting ready to walk right into one. Make sure you've got the Lord on your side. He will calm the troubled waters of your soul, protect you, and restore your situation, making you whole again!

> Isaiah 43:2—"When thou passes through the waters, I will be with thee; and through the rivers, they shall not overflow thee: when thou walkest through the fire, thou shalt not be burned, neither shall the flame kindle upon thee."

A Minute of Meditation

Can you think of a time when you were faced with a major storm in your life? How did you react to the situation? Most of us tend to think that we have total control of every situation we will ever face. The truth of the matter is, God is the one who is in control. Had it not been for His favor and blessings upon my family, honestly, I just don't know where I would be. In fact, He is the only one who really knows what the real outcome would have been. While Satan often uses the storms we go through as a reason for us to give up on God, I'm telling you, don't listen to him. If he can get in our minds and change our thoughts by placing doubt there, that is just what the devil wants to do. He seriously wants to silence the believer and remove the peace we have in our hearts from knowing and trusting Jesus. Let me just say this, when God restores you, He does a complete job! Don't give in to doubt and unbelief, just learn to trust in the God who is in control of every storm you will ever face.

Chapter 27

Facing Yet Another Storm

From the latter part of June, 2016, all the way up until the week before Christmas of that same year, we worked on trying to get our home put back together. Several of my family members stepped up and spent countless hours donating their time, labor, and own money at times to help in the restoration process. With each passing day, God showed up for us and took care of our every need. Each night when I finally made it back to my brother-in-law and sister-in-law's home, I would take a few minutes after getting a shower to stop and thank God for everything that took place during that day.

As I write about these storms, please keep in mind that Lynette and I were not the only people in our family who were walking through the same storm. Our entire community was pretty much wiped out as well as surrounding communities in our area and even several other communities in and around our state. So we were not in this thing alone. Our home church was destroyed, and many families who attend our church also lost part or everything they owned. Needless to say, by December, my stress levels had built up to the max.

My boss knew my situation as did all of my co-workers. During this six month period, every one of them helped me in some way. Some gave me money to put toward our reconstruction, others took care of my clients service needs in my absence, some brought food to my home to help feed those who were there working, and others were praying and calling on God, asking Him to help us. My boss, Philip Garlow, told me to take as long as I needed to get my home put back together and to not worry about things at the office. He assured me that if anyone called in with a need that it would be taken care of. So I am very thankful for everyone at my office who helped me get through this horrible time in my life. They are really an amazing bunch of people!

There were days when I literally worked eighteen out of a twenty-four-hour day during those six months and would get up the next morning and hit it again. We worked seven days a week from the end of June to the week of Christmas in December with several of the same people right beside us all the way. Believe me when I say I can't remember everyone who helped us out. Looking back, I wish we would have made a list of all the people by name, but that didn't happen. I guess we were consumed in our situation and didn't think far enough ahead. I have thanked many of those who helped and again I hate to mention any names in fear of offending anyone, but I do want to mention just a few individuals who sacrificed greatly in our process.

Please, please, if you helped us in any way and your name did not make this book; I sincerely want you to know that we would never be where we are today had it not been for you. My prayer is that God has richly blessed each of you a thousand times over for what you have done and given back to you as only He can!

I feel compelled to mention a few names here that worked right beside me and gave of themselves unselfishly, never asking for one thing in return. I thank God often for these individuals. They are: Forrest Deweese—my brother-in law; Howard Lavender, Jr.—my brother-in-law; Chris Deweese—my nephew; Jason Lavender—my nephew; Trey Suttle—my nephew; Steve Lucas—my first cousin; Neil Meadows—a brother-in-Christ.

I just don't have the words to say how much I appreciate this group of men. There were times when we all had so much mud on us that we could not have rolled around in a hog pen and gotten any more mud on us or smell any worse than what we smelled, but they never hesitated for one minute to do whatever was needed, and I appreciate them so very much!

So December, 2016, rolled around, and I was so tired! Everyone was tired! We all just needed a break and with Christmas coming up, we felt it was time for a break. We were able to spend time with our families celebrating the birth of our Lord and thanking Him for where He had brought us to, but I was totally drained. I told Lynette that I thought I would take a little time off after Christmas and get started back sometime after the first of the year. Something was telling me I needed to slow down, so I took a break from the daily grind of working on the house, and after Christmas I went back to work at my office.

After working all day at the office, I found myself coming home, sitting down in my recliner, and falling asleep just about as fast as I sat down. My energy levels were totally gone, I knew I was tired, but I didn't realize I was that tired. It was like my body was trying to tell me something, but I couldn't put my finger on the problem. January and February of 2017 rolled by, and with March swiftly underway, signs of springtime where starting to show up. This sparked what I thought was a resurrection in my life as I have always loved spring as you get to watch all the new life coming forth in the trees and flowers that pop their heads up out of the ground.

I came home from work on a Thursday evening, and my oldest little granddaughter came over. She loves spending time with her Grammy and Poppy, and we decided to go outside on that warm evening and do a little yard work. Nothing strenuous, we just had a pair of hedge trimmers out cutting down some ornamental grasses in the yard. My son stopped by to pick up our granddaughter, and I stayed out in my back yard finishing up our little project when suddenly I had a major fluttering in my chest. It was a very weird feeling that took my breath away and caused me to almost pass out. I had to sit down and gather my thoughts, as I really didn't know what was happening. After about fifteen minutes of sitting there on the ground, I got up and started gathering up my tools to put them away and made my way into the house.

When you live with the same woman for as many years as I've lived with Lynette, it's very hard to hide anything at all from them. She took one look at me and knew something was wrong. While I told her what had happened, like most men do, I played the situation down as if it wasn't as bad as it really was. She wanted to take me to the hospital, but I refused to go; *stupid* is all I can say about that. I told her I couldn't go to the hospital as I had a very busy day already on schedule for the following day. She was upset and worried, and I was totally being hard-headed about it and ended up getting a shower and going to bed.

Friday morning came, and I got up and went to work. I had a hard time getting up that morning, and it felt like I had run a marathon the day before. My body was hurting all over, but I made myself go to my office. That afternoon I had an appointment scheduled with a prospective client about an hour north of Charleston so I left the office around 1:30 and drove to my appointment. After my meeting, I got in my truck and started driving back down the interstate when that same fluttering in my chest hit me again. This time it was so much worse than the day before, and I wasn't even sure if I was going to make it home or not. Since my home was about halfway between where I had my meeting and my office, I decided to get off the exit and drive over to my house. When I walked in the door, Lynette took one look at me and again knew that something was wrong. While I was just about to be a total idiot, I sat down, and she insisted that we go to the hospital. My thoughts were, "This too shall pass," but the longer I sat there, the worse it got, and I finally gave in and told her to get me to the hospital, so off we went.

The next few days were a total blur to me. Things were not happening very fast at first as we sat in the emergency room for six and a half hours before they realized that just maybe I was having a heart issue. I was admitted to the hospital, and once they got me settled in, they did absolutely nothing that night but move me to a room. I guess I should have been thankful for that as at least I was able to stretch out in a bed. The following morning, I was told I needed to have a nuclear stress test for my heart as my bloodwork was showing signs of a possible problem.

With my regular cardiologist being out of town, the heart doctor that was on call at the hospital that weekend was overseeing my test that morning. After the test, he and another cardiologist were reading the results and immediately were telling me there was a problem in the front part of my heart. Without any hesitation, the two doctors were both highly suggesting and recommending a heart catheterization.

At this point, everything was starting to happen rather fast! This just couldn't be! In my mind I was trying to diagnose my own condition, and in no way did I think I could have anything wrong with my heart. Since my cardiologist was out of town, I asked the doctors who did the stress test if we could wait until Dr. Stanton got back in town on Monday morning. They felt I needed to go ahead with the catheterization but agreed that we could wait for Dr. Stanton to return. Since this was Saturday morning, I thought I would get to go home, but that was not the case. Had I gone home, I may not have gone back to the hospital, and the doctors probably knew that; I was told I could wait until Monday morning, but I would be waiting there in the hospital. My plan didn't work as I thought it would, so I found myself laying there in that hospital bed all weekend long, just waiting for Monday to come.

I was thrilled at first to see Dr. Stanton as I thought he would have some different thoughts and input in my situation. The fact is, he agreed 100 percent with the other doctors after reading the results of the stress test I had and said they would be coming to get me prepped for the heart cath. Within minutes, I was being rolled back into the Cath Lab. At this point I was pretty calm about the situation, probably because they had given me a shot of something to keep me calm during the procedure. In my mind, I was still having trouble processing everything that was taking place because it seemed to be moving along very rapidly!

The procedure didn't take very long at all. As a matter of fact, it seemed that Dr. Stanton just got in there when he pulled back a little screen and said, "We've got to get you to surgery!" He looked at the nurse and told her to get me moved to the holding area and said he would be there soon to discuss what he saw and what he was going to suggest. Suddenly the wheels in my head were spinning out of control. I knew it wasn't good, but again, while trying to diagnose my own condition, I thought he could only mean that I needed a stent, nothing more.

The news was not good! Dr. Stanton walked in with some pictures of his findings, and I was told I had multiple major blockages. Not only did I have the widow maker in the front of my heart, but I had two 95 percent blockages, two 90 percent, and one 65 percent blocked. Bypass surgery was a must, and it needed to be as quickly as they could get it scheduled. Needless to say, I felt like I was on a sinking ship with the waves crashing over my head at that moment.

With my dad passing away from a major heart attack years earlier, somehow I always knew that I would be going down that same road. However, while I was in the middle of yet another storm, I had to be thankful that God sent the warning signs He sent to give me the opportunity to even have the procedures being recommended. I'm not sure, but looking back on the situation, I sort of feel like everything that had taken place up to this point had put me into shock.

As my doctor was sharing the results of his findings, it all seemed like a very bad dream to me. Reality was setting in, and that evening and night were very long! Like the disciples we read about in Matthew, chapter 14, who were out on the sea in a ship when the storm came upon them, I sort of felt like I could understand just how they must have felt. They were being tossed with the waves, and the wind was contrary (v. 24). It was late the night before my open heart surgery, as it says in (v. 25); there I was in the fourth watch of the night when Jesus showed up in my personal storm, walking on the water. It was just me and Him in my hospital room that night when He gave me peace about my situation. Yes it was a major storm, but God let me know that He was in full control.

> Matthew 14:27—"But straightway Jesus spake unto them, saying, Be of good cheer; it is I; be not afraid."

A Minute of Meditation

If you would, pause right here for a few minutes and reflect back over your life. If you've lived long enough, I know for certain that you can think of a time when you received some news you more than likely was never expecting to hear! Think about how you reacted in that particular moment. Did it put you in shock? Did worry cross your mind? Maybe the news hit a nerve you never even realized you had. My friends, there are different kinds of storms that come up in life, and we all have to face them. Just as the disciples were faced with fear in the darkest part of the night when the storm suddenly came upon them, we too often find ourselves facing moments of uncontrollable fear, the kind that only God can remove and replace with the special peace that He alone can give. Where are you today? Did you just come out of a storm, or are you presently in the middle of a storm? If things happen to be going along pretty good right now, buckle up; you will soon be heading right into another unexpected situation soon! It's just a part of life.

Chapter 28

Voices and Choices

One of my favorite places on the map to visit is Daytona Beach, Florida. While I've been blessed to visit the shoreline and beaches of Virginia, North Carolina, South Carolina, California, Washington State, Alaska, and several of the Hawaiian Islands to mention a few, I have to say that the beaches down in Florida seem to call out my name more than any of them. There's just nothing like pulling up a chair down by the edge of the surf and watching the tide roll in and out. The sound of the oceans waves crashing on a sandy beach are one of the most relaxing and peaceful things I believe I've ever experienced. For me, it's been a place that God just seems to speak to my heart.

Knowing the Master of the sea personally make these moments very special to me. I've come to realize that like the ocean tides that are constantly on the move, like the waves that never stop rolling into the shoreline, so is life. Life keeps moving on and often in many different directions. Even though we are tossed around and our spirit sometimes is restless, we grow as individuals as we move along experiencing and living life. We learn that when we fall, we have to get up, dust ourselves off, and start putting one foot in front of the other again. Sometimes while walking along, we find ourselves in deep, dark places. Then there are those moments when we struggle just trying to get up the mountain we've been climbing. For me, when things start to cave in all around me, a trip to the beach seems to call out to me as I just need a little wave therapy to get my mind clear and refocused on all of the blessings God has so often given me.

Growing up in the mountains of West Virginia offered so much to me as a kid. However, the mountain terrain is much different from the flat sandy shorelines of the south. Every year, those who worked in the coal mines were granted their vacations at the same time. Since it took a whole crew of men to get the job done, rather than trying to run multiple shifts shorthanded, most of the mines would shut down at the same time to allow all their employees to get away for a vacation. The roads going south would be full of West Virginia coal miners and their families heading to the beaches for some fun in the sun! My dad didn't really care much for the sand, but he did enjoy sitting out on the balcony of the motel, reading his Bible and listening to the sound of the ocean. He also knew how much we enjoyed it, so it was just a common place for us to visit for our summer vacations. I'm sure after working in a dark, deep hole in the ground day in and day out, the sunshine would look and feel good to a miner. I guess that's why so many of them went south.

Just as the sound of the waves crashing on the seashore always seemed to calm my nerves and relax my mind, there were a lot of places I found where I could get tuned into the voice of God. Back in the mountains of West Virginia, I always enjoyed sitting down in a stand of tall pine trees. As the wind softly blows through the needles of a high, lofty pine tree, I always found that to be very relaxing as well. There are areas across America where pine trees dominate the forest. Unlike it is in the South where you see nothing but pine trees, West Virginia has a lot of hard woods with pines scattered throughout the timber line. For those of us who live in the mountains, spending time in the great outdoors is just something we do a lot of. Much like the wave therapy you get at the beach, a good o'l mountain trout stream with clear, cool flowing water can offer some great therapy of its own. Most of us enjoy time out by the stream or in the woods hunting, pretty much year round. There have been many occasions while sitting under a long-needle pine tree or beside a swift-moving mountain trout stream that I've heard God's voice speaking to me. I've always found that being out in nature is a great place to connect with God.

Far too often, friends, we just go about living life and fail to take time to enjoy the little things that God blesses us with. We are too busy to enjoy the simple things. God created nature for a purpose, I believe its purpose is to give us a chance to see God in a very special way. The world is a beautiful place, and nature is full of all different types of beauty; however, if you never take time to get out in it, you're not going to get the full effect of it. The same principal applies in relation to living a life in Christ. If you never spend time alone with God and never stop to listen for His voice, it's highly likely that you are not going to experience the fullness He has in mind for you in this life. This world is a beautiful place, but, my friends, the world has absolutely nothing to offer you without Christ living within your heart. Things often seem dark and complicated when you're walking along on this journey without Christ. It's when, and only when, you accept Christ into your life that you really begin to live and see the beauty in God's creation as it should be. Learning to let God take control and direct our steps is so important.

There are all kinds of voices in the world around us, and they speak to us every day. Growing up, we spend a lot of time with our friends and the conversations we have as well as the things we do, often identify the path we are walking on. Our parents give us instructions and advice; sometimes we listen; and sometimes the words they speak fall on deaf ears. The future of our success as individuals can be defined early on; however, it is going to depend on whether or not we take the instructions and advice given and apply it to our everyday living. God speaks to us in many different ways as well. His living Word, the scriptures, speak to us if we will take the time to read it. He speaks to us through preachers He has called to minister to our needs, but if we never attend a local assembly or ever tune into a gospel radio or television broadcast, we are not going to receive the message God is trying to relay to us. I mentioned how He speaks to me through nature, but if I'm not spending time listening for His voice, I'm simply not going to hear it!

On the other hand, Satan's voice seems to be very loud and noticeable in the world we are living in today. It's so loud that it has become very distracting. It seems the more true Christ followers try to share the love of Jesus with the world, Satan chimes in louder than ever trying to silence the voice of truth! Things that use to be considered wrong are now viewed as being right and very acceptable in society. Lifestyles that are defined as unacceptable in the eyes of Christ, according to the scriptures, are now in the forefront of just about everything we see. From the news media, to the big screen, in every magazine, every type of advertisement, down to the local newspapers and every source of social media, Satan's voice is being heard and his ways are being visualized right in front of our eyes while the world is trying to silence the voice of God. Things have drastically changed and not for the good!

My life is no different from yours just as your life is no different from mine, as far as the many different voices we hear while on this journey. There is something or someone calling out to us constantly. Country music legend, George Jones, recorded a song one time that was titled, "Choices." The song started off with these words:

I've had choices
Since the day that I was born.

There were voices
That told me right from wrong.
If I had listened,
No, I wouldn't be here today,
Living and dying
With the choices I made.

While we hear the voices that are speaking to us, the most important thing is how we react to what those voices are saying to us. More importantly, the decisions we make in how we respond to what these voices are calling out for us to do can make a huge difference in the overall outcome for our lives. I'm talking about our lives here on earth as well as the eternal life we will all have in the future. Much like the tides of the oceans, we are being challenged and pulled in many different directions. We are tossed about in the waves and bear the scars of being thrown into the rocks along the shoreline. If we are not careful, we will find ourselves drifting along like a ship with no captain at the helm. Today, you have a choice. You can decide to follow Jesus, or you can choose to listen to the voice of Satan. I'm here to tell you, not only will Satan try to silence you, but he will use every way possible to get your sidetracked in life. The danger of that is this; if we fail to follow and listen to the voice of God now, we may find ourselves standing before Him in eternity to hear Him say, "Sorry, I never knew you, depart from me," and hell will be our eternal destiny! It's something to really think about!

> Psalm 29:3–4—"The voice of the Lord is upon the waters: the God of glory thundereth: the Lord is upon many waters. The voice of the Lord is powerful; the voice of the Lord is full of majesty."

A Minute of Meditation

Pause for a moment and think about all the voices that call out to you on a daily basis. Can you think of a time when you know for certain that both God and Satan were calling out to you? It would be crazy to think for a minute that there was not a battle going on in your mind. How did you react? What was your response? Did you make a decision to go God's way with the situation, or did you cave into Satan? My friends, God wants to use you for His glory! Satan's goal is to silence you, to defeat, devour, and destroy you! Train your ear to listen for the voice of God and follow His instructions. One day you will be glad you did!

Chapter 29

Learning to Lean

When a little baby is born, it has no choice; it must depend on someone else to feed it, change its diapers, put clean clothes on it, and cover it up to keep it warm and cozy. Before it learns to talk, its mother or dad have to try to figure out what is hurting it when it cries uncontrollably and do what they can to comfort it. As time rolls along, that newborn baby soon realizes if it cries, it will get some attention, so what does it do? It cries! Why? If you've never noticed that, let me encourage you to start paying attention when you are around the next newborn baby you come in contact with. It is just a natural thing that occurs in the life of a newborn child.

Watching my boys grow up was an exciting thing for me. I was disappointed if I was not home when they crossed another milestone, things like seeing them take their first steps or hearing them say their first word or seeing them doing something new like being able to stack blocks on top of each other as they developed their motor skills. Of course, before they started walking, they first had to learn to crawl, and before they would take off walking on their own, they learned to pull up to a coffee table and lean on that table for support. Soon, Lynette and I would work with them and encourage them to put one foot in front of the other, and before we knew it, they were walking on their own.

Much like a child who is learning to walk, life at best can cause us to be a little shaky. When we crawl, we are down on our hands and knees and have a little more stability about us; but when we have to learn to balance ourselves and walk at the same time, it takes a little more skill and effort. All these things we learn from a very young age. After we have learned to lean, we soon learn to balance ourselves, and before we know it, we are on our way. The journey has begun.

For some children, learning how to walk is a real challenge. Others, like our youngest little granddaughter, take off walking before they are eight months old and never look back. Why is that? Well, I'm not really sure, but I think it is a confidence thing. If you watch for it, you can see it. Some kids are just determined that they are going to learn how to do something, and they will work and work until they are able to accomplish things on their own. I can't remember anything about the days when I first learned to crawl or even when I took my first steps. Without a doubt, someone had to work with me and help me and based on my experience of being a dad, I'm certain that I fell a lot before I gained enough confidence to keep my balance and keep putting one foot out in front of the other until I could make my way across the floor. Thank God for those who have helped us along the way!

Back on November 4, 1977, my middle sister Joyce gave birth to her first son Jason. I don't know if you've ever thought about all the hats you wear in life, but if you ever stop and list them, you will find you wear many. One of the favorite hats I've worn is that of "Uncle Tony"! Each time my two sisters gave birth to their children, it made my heart jump with joy as I knew my title as an uncle had just expanded. I loved them all equally and would do anything in the world for any one of them. After Lynette's brother Wally got married, she and I were blessed with another nephew and another niece on her side of the family, and we've enjoyed life with all of them! We now get to enjoy life, watching their kids growing up while we just keep getting older.

Watching all these kids grow up and having a small part in each of their lives was fun and exciting for me. As each one of my nephews and nieces learned to crawl, then walk, and learn to talk and develop into young men and women who eventually ended up getting married and having children of their own, I was proud of them all and always enjoyed watching them as their children started through the whole process of learning to do all the same things I had watched them do. The circle of life friends is an amazing thing to watch, and for me, family means everything. The saddest part is how fast life really does pass by.

While learning to lean on those who love you should be the first thing we do; it seems that as we grow up and become an adult, we become independent. I know that is the natural progression and the way it's supposed to happen, but as I mentioned in the last chapter, there are voices that call out to us and if we fall into the trap and get out of step with God as well as with those who love us the most, often the end results can be very costly.

If we lived in a perfect world, we would never have to experience bad things. If we would all be sold out to Christ and truly follow Him daily and trust Him for everything we have need of, then just maybe we could avoid many of the bad things that come our way. This chapter has been a difficult one to write, but I really felt compelled to share this story with you in hopes that it may help someone else. With the blessings of my sister Joyce and her husband Howard, I want to share some of the struggles that we have had as a family. As you will see, we've all had to lean on Christ and to this day, there are still a lot of unanswered questions in our minds.

Very early on the morning of May 8, 2019, my phone started ringing. It was laying on the nightstand beside my bed, and when I rolled over to answer it, I saw my sister's name on the screen.

Immediately I knew something had to be wrong for her to be calling me that early in the morning. Upon answering the call, my sister was in a panic; she was crying uncontrollably, and she said; "Tony, it's Joyce, he's gone! Jason is gone!" It was a call I never ever wanted to get, but somehow I always knew that it was going to happen. A life that began on November 4, 1977, suddenly was over.

It is my prayer and the prayers of my sister and brother-in-law that maybe this story will help someone else who may be experiencing a similar problem in your own family. While my nephew Jason is no longer with us, I'm certain that he would want me to be sharing his story in an effort to keep someone else from going down the path that he went down.

Jason was raised in a Christian home by two godly parents who dearly loved him. He had two siblings, his brother Chad and his sister Angela, all of whom had a lot of love for each other and a great home life. As a lot of kids do, Jason was a follower from a very young age. Other kids could talk him into trying things or doing things, and he would do them! He started experimenting with things at a young age that he knew he shouldn't have been doing, but needless to say, he did them. One thing lead to another and by the time he got into college, he had drifted a long way away from the way he was brought up and rather than asking for help, his pride got the best of him.

He soon got married, and he and his wife had two beautiful kids! He was the proud father of his daughter who was born first, then along came his son, and Jason loved each one of his children dearly! Unfortunately, his marriage ended in a divorce, and from that point on Jason's life began spiraling out of control. Over the years, he and I had a lot of conversations about this as he was convinced he was a failure. He was heartbroken that it happened; but instead of leaning on God for direction, he dug the hole he was in deeper and deeper, as he was searching for happiness and something to fill the void that was now in his life.

As much as he tried to hide his problems, he just couldn't do it. He would get himself out of one mess and walk right into another, all at the same time. Many in our family tried our best to help him out. I didn't have all the answers, but I always tried to point him back to the Cross. He had my full support and knew it, and regardless of what he ever did; he knew I loved him! Listen, friends, you can love someone and you can talk until you are blue in the face, but until they are ready to do something about their situation, nothing is going to change until they are ready to change! I just knew if he was going to ever recover, he had to turn everything over to the Lord and ask Him for the help he needed to move on.

Like many places around the United States, our little state of West Virginia is no different. Most families here have been touched in some way from various addictions, but we have lead the nation in the opioid addiction epidemic, due to doctors writing prescriptions and making opioids so easy for individuals to get. When these things hit the streets, it became a pure epidemic for many people in and around all of our communities. With Jason being a follower, he fell prey to those who claimed to be his friends. While he thought they were trying to help him get over his problems, what he didn't realize was how addicting the things he was experimenting with would be. Over time, he found himself in and out of jail, in and out of the hospital, and constantly in financial trouble. Keeping a job became very difficult, and in many cases impossible, because of his addictions, but with all the love we had, we continued to do everything in our power to try to help him get himself back to some kind of a normal life.

I watched as all he was doing had a major grip on his life. I saw the heartbreak, worry, and disappointment he brought on his mother and dad, and from the outside looking in; my heart was breaking for his children. I was troubled inside as I was searching for ways that I could help him in his situation. I finally met up with the fact that taking all these matters to God in prayer and giving them all to Him was just about all that was left to do. I would like to tell you that giving all of this to God was exactly what I did, but like we so often do, I felt the need to pick up the things I left on the altar for Jason and start trying to do what I could to help him. Somehow I finally got Jason to agree to get himself some help. He had landed in jail again and was sent to a facility temporarily until we could get him into a rehab program. Without a doubt, God worked out the details for us, and we were successful in getting him in a state rehab facility where he began his recovery process.

Fast forward and after spending over fourteen very hard and difficult months in the rehab facility, Jason was released to yet another facility back in Charleston, which was a lot closer to home where he spent another year. He had to have a job within two weeks of getting to the group home where he would be living, and things were starting to take a very positive turn for him at this point. Feeling as if things were working out, it was great to see the positive changes that were taking place in his life.

Time marched on, but it was evident that everything Jason had been through was very difficult for him to experience and endure. He thanked me over and over for helping him get to where he was, and as I always did, I continued to encourage him by pointing him to the Cross and letting him know that he just had to lean on Christ for the direction he needed for his future. You may or may not know anything at all about drug and alcohol addiction, but one thing is for certain: when it gets a grip on you, it's not something that you are going to beat very easily. During the next few years, Jason lost several friends to drug overdoses, and while he was doing well, when this happened, he would fall off the wagon again and start using again as this was his way of trying to escape the pain and loss he was going through.

Understanding the kind of addictions that Jason battled for many years was hard for me. One reason is I've elected to stay away from drugs, and at fifty-nine years old, I can honestly say that I've never tasted alcohol of any kind. I've been around it, I've seen what it does to people, I've smelled it, and if the smell of it makes me sick, I always knew that I would be the one with my head hanging over a toilet throwing up if I ever drank it, so it was water or coke for me. A very important lesson I learned, though, while trying to help my nephew is the fact that you need to understand how easy it is to have an addiction. Please understand that an addiction can be something as simple as overeating, it could be pornography which is something a lot of people struggle with, you may have a money addiction that consumes your life and causes you to work day and night to accomplish the things you want to accomplish in this life. For some, just wanting to be accepted by the crowd can cause them to do things that bring on addictions. It never bothered me that I didn't drink beer with my friends or experiment with different kinds of drugs. I could drink a coke and be perfectly happy! I could see where I was not considered to be one of the popular people in the crowd, but after seeing what these things were doing to my friends, I made the decision that I didn't want to be part of that crowd anymore. It didn't mean they were not my friends, it just meant that I could not relate to the things they were doing, and I would find other ways to entertain myself like going fishing with my dad or just hanging out with him.

Whatever you battle, my friends, until you learn to lean on Jesus and learn to lay all of your problems at His feet and not pick them back up and try to carry them on your own again, you are never going to win the battle! Looking back, I've asked myself over and over what I could have done differently that would have made a difference in our family's situation. If Jason would have listened to all of us who loved him unconditionally and could have been strong enough to walk away from those who brought him down, things may have been different. I wish I could tell you that Jason beat his addictions, but all the years of the alcohol and drug abuse finally took a toll on his health and ultimately contributed to his early death. While he seemed to be doing so much better, the hidden damage was done. Jason had assured me that his heart was right with God and he had peace about that, but his life was shortened by the long-term choices he made. Only God knows how things would have been different had Jason just learned to lean on Christ long ago and quit trying to fight his battles on his own.

While writing this chapter I was reminded of all the friends I've lost to drug and alcohol abuse. I can think of so many special families that my wife and I know who have had to deal with the sudden loss of a son or daughter, a brother or sister, a dad or mom because of addictions that had a grip on their loved ones and ultimately ended up taking their life at an early age. Satan will use these things, friends, to try to defeat us. All we can do is give it our best shot! I tried my best with my nephew, and when we lost him, Satan was all over me once again in an attempt to silence me, but I have to cling to the blessed hope that God's Word gives us and because of Jason's faith in God, I have to believe that I will see him again.

As I was struggling with things that morning on May 8, 2019, a gentleman patted me on the back and tried to bring some comfort to my hurting heart by saying, "You know, Tony, sometimes I think God looks down and says, enough is enough; my child has had enough!" I've thought about that a lot since that day, and as much as I would like to bring Jason back, I do believe he had suffered long enough. God knew the struggles, he knew the heartache and pain that Jason had been living in down here, and

I have to believe that God took him out of his troubles. Friends, there is hope in Jesus. Even when everything seems hopeless and hope is hard to find, we have to lean on Him and trust that He will see us through every trial we will ever face!

Satan will use situations like this to try to silence us, friends. I felt somewhat defeated once again in my life when the reality of losing my nephew settled in. There were thoughts that crossed my mind, making me feel as if Satan was winning the battle. As hard as I tried to help Jason, the devil was trying to convince me that he won the battle in Jason's life. Now that he was gone, I was feeling like a failure myself in my own personal life. Why would this happen? What good could possibly come out of this situation? Did I do everything I could have? The bottom line is this: God said it was enough! I knew I couldn't let this defeat me even though my heart was broken; but being one who has had to lean on Christ throughout my entire life, Satan was still hard at work on me. I was reminded of all the advice I had given to Jason about leaning on Christ and realized that I needed to get my eyes turned toward the same Cross I had pointed Jason to so many times. I also had to remind Satan that Jason belonged to Christ and was now an overcomer! His days of leaning on Christ were over; he's now in the presence of Christ forever!

> 1 John 4:4—"Ye are of God, little children, and
> have overcome them: because greater is he that is
> in you, than he that is in the world."

A Minute of Meditation

I wish this chapter would have had a different ending, but unfortunately, life doesn't always end well. When we give in to our circumstances and fail to totally lean on Christ for the direction we need for each day, friends, things just aren't going to end well. As much as God wants us to lay our burdens and cares upon Him, if we fail to do so, we are basically telling God that we can handle things on our own. You and I know that is not the case. No matter how strong we think we are as individuals, how rooted we may think we are in our faith in God, regardless of the love and support that our family and friends offer us, Satan is never going to let up with his efforts of trying to destroy us. We can't fight our battles on our own; we need the help of God, and the sooner we realize that, the better off we will be. Today, you may find yourself in the same position that our family was in. You may be facing the same challenges with someone you love with all your heart, and you see the grip that addiction has on their life. I would like to encourage you by saying, don't give up! Keep praying, keep caring, keep loving and showing that child, brother, sister, husband, wife, mother, father, or friend what a special person they are. Whatever you do, don't let Satan silence you. Use your voice and the circumstances you have faced or are presently facing to help others.

Chapter 30

2020 Vision

I never dreamed that in my lifetime I would ever see the things that are happening here in America that I am seeing today! As I'm writing this chapter, we are a little more than halfway through the year. So far, the year of 2020 has been a very eventful year! Not a year of exciting events, but one that we can mark and will remember as an interesting year or possibly an unbelievable year! Many of the events that are taking place are not only happening here in the United States of America, but they are worldwide events, things that are affecting the entire human race.

It's another election year here in America, which is a very important time for our nation. In my opinion, it is a very critical time, not only for America, but for the entire world! The upcoming presidential election is one that I feel in my heart will either give America one more chance to get things right, or it will be the end of the greatest nation in the world. Either way, I'm of the opinion that it is all in God's perfect plan. I'm going to remain as positive as I possibly can and trust God in the process. I feel if I do that then everything will be alright.

This country is the greatest country in the entire world. How do I know that? Well, everyone wants to move to America. Those in other countries have seen how blessed we have been as a nation here in the United States, and they want what we have. If I was on the outside looking in a few years ago, I would certainly want what everyone in America has had; however, the longer we go, the worse it is getting. Is it because we have allowed other cultures to move here and bring their belief systems here that were not working where they came from? Or, is it that we Americans no longer have a clear vision of how blessed we are as a nation, and we actually think that the way of life that others are bringing here is better than what we actually have? I'm not exactly sure what it is, but my opinion is that we are losing our sight!

Once a nation that valued, believed in, and included God in everything we did; we are now moving farther and farther away from God! Hatred is replacing love, war is replacing peace, and we are heading toward a controlled government where the freedom as we've known it, the freedom that so many have fought and died for, is soon going to be a thing of the past. The young minds of America are being destroyed and swayed into believing that there is a better way, but the better way will soon only be in our rearview mirrors, something we will only remember and wish we had back!

If we were really "One Nation Under God," maybe we would try to listen to what God had to say about faith, hope, and charity. Here is what 1 Corinthians 13:4–13 from the Bible has to say:

> Charity suffereth long, and is kind; charity envieth not; charity vaunteth not itself, is not puffed up, Doth not behave itself unseemly, seeketh not her own, is not easily provoked, thinketh not evil; Rejoiceth not in iniquity, but rejoiceth in the truth; Beareth all things, believeth all things, hopeth all things, endureth all things. Love never faileth: but whether there be prophecies, they shall fail; whether there be tongues, they shall cease; whether there be knowledge, it shall vanish away. For we know in part, and we prophesy in part. But when

that which is perfect is come, then that which is in part shall be done away. When I was a child, I spake as a child, I understood as a child, I thought as a child, but when I became a man, I put away childish things. For now we see through a glass darkly; but then face to face: now I know in part; but then shall I know even as also I am known. And now abideth faith, hope, charity, these three; but the greatest of these is charity.

I'm beginning to think that people are totally losing their minds. We've gone from being a fairly peaceful nation to looking like other nations around the world that we used to see news reports of where people were fighting in the streets, burning vehicles, and blowing up buildings. Racism has become a major issue across America once again. One would think that we could get over this problem, but for some reason the belief that different races possess distinct characteristics, abilities, or qualities that distinguish them as inferior or superior to one another has taken over the minds of many. We are all a creation of God, and while some have abilities that may be greater than others, we are all important to society and in the eyes of God. We can all have a positive impact on the world that we live in regardless of our race or ethnic status!

Rioting, looting, and ransacking beautiful cities across America as well as physically destroying many historical monuments around our nation has been another major problem that we've seen in 2020. Some folks decided we needed to change the names of various products that have been around for years and built a very successful business around a brand that was established many, many years ago. There are those who felt that some of the professional sports teams across America needed to change their names because the names they have had for years is now offending someone. The rioting and looting has totally gotten out of control, with the streets of our great country filled with polluted messes left behind. Our law and civil enforcement have become ineffective, and we now have a movement to defund these very important agencies here in America. What are we thinking? Can we not see where this is going to take us?

Another issue that the whole world has had to deal with in 2020 is the COVID-19 virus. It has recently been estimated that over 630,000 lives have been lost as a result of this worldwide pandemic, with thousands being infected daily and the death toll still climbing. It was originally reported that this virus first surfaced in China and has since spread completely around the world. Some don't see it as anything to be concerned with; however, if you get a chance to talk to someone who has lost a love one to this horrible virus or possibly talk to someone who had it and survived it, maybe those who don't see it as anything serious would change their minds. Regardless of where the virus started, the whole world has to deal with it. Will they ever get a vaccine to treat the symptoms of this virus? Will there ever be a cure for it? We can only hope there will be. There are billions of dollars going into the research for the answers to this problem. The economy of the entire world is suffering as a result of this pandemic, and our hospitals are maxed out with the medical doctors and nurses doing all they can due to sustain life for those who are clinging to life. One by one, people are dying from what has been described by many as a horrible death.

Could it be that Satan is using all the events of the present day in which we are living to silence the voice of the Christians, those who believe in Christ? I mean, after all, here in America we've been forced to shut down pretty much everything for lengthy periods of time, including our churches and synagogues. Is there a possibility that Satan could be using the racial problems that have resurfaced in such a horrible way to silence the voice of reason and love in our country? Could it be that the liberal movement we are seeing is something that Satan is going to use to try to silence the voice of reason and truth? What if all the events of today are the beginning of the end? Could it be that God is allowing these things to happen to get our attention? It could be that these current events that are taking place are being used by God to strengthen those who say they believe in Christ to prepare them for what is to come? I think all of these questions are worthy of giving them a little thought!

Regardless of what you believe, don't be taken by surprise! I don't claim to have all the answers, but I have read the Bible from cover to cover and spent my entire life in church, listening to ministers preaching the Word and teachers teaching the Word. I would like to recommend or suggest that you get yourself a Bible and read it. Why? Well, first off, it is important to understand the events that are going to take place and how they are going to include you! It is also very interesting to see that many of the things that you read about that were written and recorded thousands of years ago are actually taking place right in front of your eyes today. It's important that you live and have a peaceful life, but it's even more important that you are prepared for your future. While Satan would like to silence your voice and cause you to become deaf to the truth of the Word and blind to what is to come, God wants you to have an abundant life and the hope and promise of an eternal future that includes a place called heaven for those who believe.

Don't allow your vision to be blurred by the events that are taking place all around you. Ask God to give you a clear 20/20 vision in 2020 and learn what it means to walk with God and trust Him with your life. He has a promised future for the believers as well as those who choose not to believe the truth. What will be your choice?

Matthew 24:6–14 says:

> And ye shall hear of wars and rumors of wars: see that ye be not troubled: for all these things must come to pass, but the end is not yet. For nation shall rise against nation, and kingdom against kingdom: and there shall be famines, and pestilence, (COVID-19), and earthquakes, in divers places. All of these are the beginning of sorrows. Then shall they deliver you up to be afflicted, and shall kill you: and ye shall be hated of all nations for my name's sake. And then shall many be offended, and shall betray one another, and shall hate one another. And many false prophets shall rise, and shall deceive many. And because iniquity shall abound, the love of many shall wax cold. But he that shall endure unto the end, the same shall be saved. And this gospel of the kingdom shall be preached in all the world for a witness unto all nations; and then shall the end come.

A Minute of Meditation

I seriously don't think you have to be a Bible scholar or a professor with a PhD to understand what the scriptures are telling us and showing us about the day in which we are living in. You simply need to ask God to give you wisdom about what you are reading and learn to exercise your faith. Everyone has a measure of faith—everyone! When you mention faith, immediately there are some who associate it only with God, and they will blatantly tell you they don't believe in God or *faith*! While they may not believe in God, I promise you that they exercise faith every day of their lives; we all do. We put the key in the ignition of our cars, and we have faith that it is going to start. We put the car in drive, and we have faith that it is going to get us to where we are going. We flip the light switch to the on position, and we have the faith that the light is going to come on. We open our eyes in the morning, and we have faith that we are going to be able to see the light of another day. However, my friends, if we are not careful, we will allow the current events of today to distort or even destroy our vision entirely. Our chances of believing the truth are swiftly passing by and will soon be a thing of the past. Whatever you do, don't allow Satan to silence you or trick you into not believing there is a God who cares for you and has a promised future for you. May we all get focused on the things that are important that hold great eternal value!

Chapter 31

It's Not Over Yet

I f you are still reading this book, I want to personally thank you! As a kid growing up and all the way through school, I seriously hated to read books or write any kind of report or paper; however, writing a book has always been on my bucket list. One positive thing the past few years has given to me has been the opportunity to accomplish this task. I want to thank God for giving the direction and for keeping my thoughts together as well as keeping me focused as I've attempted this. This has basically been a picture of my journey through life, and I have taken you from the beginning of my life all the way to the present day. But life is not over yet! While this is the last chapter of this book, I already have a desire to try to write another book, and with God's help, I hope to accomplish that in my lifetime sometime before my life is over.

The events I have written about are all connected to real-life situations that have taken place in my personal life. We all have similar struggles that we deal with daily on this journey of life, and even though they may be different struggles, for the most part, we go through a lot of the same valleys. It's unfortunate that many people are not blessed to live a long life. Even worse than that, it's unfortunate that we don't listen to the voice of God any better than we do throughout our lives. For those who have lived fifty-nine years like me or maybe even longer than that, we can all look back and see the mistakes we've made, and we all know we could have done a better job at making a difference in the world in which we live. There's always something we could have done differently that may have resulted in a more positive outcome. The problem is, we allow the voice of Satan to drown out the voice of God, and we fail to accomplish all we could, or we fail to become the person that God wants us to become because of that.

With all this said, I would like to direct your attention to a man in the Bible by the name of David. David was very much like you and me in that he had a lot of struggles in life. I love reading the book of Psalms and David is attributed to writing 73 of the 150 chapters of this great book in the scriptures. In Psalm 139, David writes and describes the everlasting presence and power of God. The chapter begins with, "O Lord, thou hast searched me, and known me." (Please take a few minutes and read the entire 139th chapter of the wonderful book of Psalms)!

Throughout my entire life, like David, I too can say that God has always been with me. He has searched me and, above all, He knows everything there is to know about me. He knows my strengths and certainly knows my weaknesses, and yet He still loves me. When I read this great chapter of God's Word today, I'm reminded that life for me is not over yet. I'm reminded that apparently there is still something that God wants me to do, and if you are reading this, you need to understand that there are things that you can do that could possibly have an eternal impact on the lives of others.

David wrote in the last two verses of Psalm 139 these words: "Search me, O God, and know my heart: try me, and know my thoughts: And see if there be any wicked way in me, and lead me in the way everlasting."

The chapter began by saying, "O Lord, thou hast searched me, and known me." Understand this friends, God knows each and every one of us. He knows each time we fall or fail Him, and He knows about the good things we do and when we are standing strong and tall. He is with us every step of the journey, and He has promised to never leave us! What a thought! When you read what David wrote in this chapter of God's Word, you can feel his concerns. Like David, we need to pause today and ask God to search us and know our hearts and thoughts. We need to ask God to show us if there are any wicked ways within us, and if so, ask Him to remove those wicked ways and thoughts and to guide our steps throughout the remainder of our journey so that we can live a life that will leave a positive mark on this world and in the lives of everyone we come in contact with.

If you have never accepted Christ in your heart and life, maybe you have read this book and you can relate to the struggles that I have shared with you about my own personal life situations. Possibly as you read the scripture verses I shared at the end of each chapter, it may have been the very first time you read those words. My prayer is that all the scriptures I've shared have caused you to see that the promises of God are real, and they apply to you and your real-life situations as you are walking along on your journey. Yes, it's true, we all have struggles, we face temptations, walk through some deep dark valleys, and experience trial after trial. It's a fact that Satan is out to destroy us all! That is a very true statement, and he wants to *silence* all of us! While we still have breath and life in these earthly bodies, we need to understand that God is not through with us yet. It's not over yet! The battles will continue, and sometimes we may find ourselves in an all-out war; just remember, all these things are a part of God's great big plan for our lives. David reminds us in Psalm 140, the very next chapter of the book of Psalms, of some things that are important for our survival. He says: "Deliver me, O Lord," "Keep me, O Lord," "Preserve me," and "Hear the voice of my supplications, O Lord"!

If there is ever a time that we need the Lord, it is in this day and age in which we are living today! Do you know him? Have you ever given any thought as to how simple it is to know God, or has it always seemed to be complicated to you? I want to leave you with these simple truths.

1. We are *all* sinners. It's not a secret; when we were born into this world, we arrived a pure sinner! Yes, as a baby we were totally innocent, but as life went on, each of us finally came to a point when we realized that some of the things we were doing were not the right things to be doing. We discovered the difference between right and wrong and that is when that sin nature reared its ugly head and showed the true evidence that we are *all* sinners! Romans 3:23 confirms this for us: *"For all have sinned and come short of the glory of God"*

2. Because of the sin that occurred all the way back in the very beginning of time in the garden of Eden, what God had created to be a good and wonderful thing suddenly became cursed by the darkness of Satan. Man and woman who had been created in the image of God failed to follow some simple directions. Because of their weakness, they failed, and therefore, death was passed to us all. Romans 6:23 explains it this way: *"For the wages of sin is DEATH, but the gift of God is eternal life through Jesus Christ our Lord."*

It's like this, if you work a job, you earn a wage for the work you do. The wages we earn for the sins we commit in our lifetime is *death*! God honestly had a different idea in mind, but because of the disobedience of the first man and woman who were created by God, the plan changed and death was passed to all mankind a result of man's sin. However, that's not the end of the story! Yes, it's true, the wages of sin is death; but the good news is this, you just read it: "The gift of God is eternal life through Jesus Christ our Lord." (This is the second half of Romans 6:23, and it presents a very positive solution to the *sin problem*)!

So what about this gift of eternal life? What is it all about? How does one take possession of such an amazing thing? First of all, it is very important to understand that God is not out to destroy you! It's not in His nature to condemn you because of *sin*, in fact you can read in 2 Peter 3:9 that *"God is not willing that any should perish, but that all should come to repentance."* Yes *sin* is a problem, but *repentance* is the solution to that problem! In John 3:17 you can read this: *"For God sent not his Son into the world to CONDEMN the world; but that the world through him might be saved."* So as you can see, God does not want anybody to go to the horrible place that is described as *hell*. He's not out to get you and point out all the sin you're involved in; that's just not what God is all about. Friends, the fact is, we are allowing sin to control us and failure to do something about it is what is sending people to hell by the thousands! You see, within each living person, we all have something that is built into our DNA; it is called a "conscious." Once we get to the age of accountability, that conscious kicks in automatically, and suddenly we are aware of the things that are right and things that are considered to be wrong. Please understand something here, while the world has many different definitions of how we define right and wrong, I sincerely believe that down deep inside of each of us, we can distinguish the truth between what is truly right and what is truly wrong! However, the battle for your eternal soul is for real! God's plan for you to escape hell will not cost you a dime, but it did cost His Son Jesus his life!

3. This thought about the *gift* of eternal life continues. My friends, a gift is not a gift until someone receives it. Let's

take another look for just a minute at the book of John. We will go to chapter 3, verse 16. This is the greatest expression of God's love that we find in the Bible! As you read this, quietly think about what the verse is saying.

"For God so loved the world, that he gave his only begotten Son, that whosoever believeth in him should not perish, but have everlasting life."

You see, some say that God made a mistake when He allowed sin to enter the garden. I don't think that is the truth of the matter at all. I think He wanted to see how obedient and how thankful those He created would be. Nevertheless, it caused God to feel bad enough that He felt it was necessary to provide a solution to the sin problem! His solution included His *only begotten Son*, Jesus! *Please* just let this sink in. Think about His *love* for just a moment longer. I am in no way suggesting that God made a mistake; however, if in fact He did, He was man enough to come up with a solution that I really don't think any of us would ever consider doing. Sin creates things like hatred, and believe me, as you read what God is all about, there are those in this world today who literally hate God! So how hard would it be for you to give your only begotten son to become *sin's ultimate sacrifice* for the sins of the entire world that doesn't even like you? Well, it is a kind of love that is nearly impossible to imagine, but I can tell you that it is real.

4. Receiving this gift. It's as simple as this—You *ask*, you *believe*, and you *receive*! You may ask, "Tony, is it really as simple as that?" My response to that question is, yes, it is that easy. In Romans 10:9–10, you can read the instructions that we are given as to how we can receive the gift of eternal life. Here is what it says:

170

If thou, (this means you); If you will confess with your mouth the Lord Jesus and if you will believe in your heart that God hath raised him from the dead, then you SHALL be saved. For with the heart man believes unto righteousness; and with the mouth confession is made unto salvation.

You see, we first need to ask God to forgive us for our unbelief and confess our sins! Then we need to believe that Jesus is the *one* who came to die for the sins of the whole world and believe that this includes our individual sins! When you do this, my friends, salvation will come to your house.

You need to understand something here, the scripture says: "*Whosoever believeth on Him shall not be ashamed.*"

Surely after you have read all that I've shared about how much God loves, you could never be ashamed! There's no reason to be ashamed; we just need to be thankful for the provisions He has made for us to experience not only a better life here on earth, but He has also planned for a wonderful future for us in heaven!

You may ask, "How can we know this for certain?" Well, three verses down in the book of Romans, chapter 10, verse 13, this is the written *guarantee!* Think about this: "*For whosoever shall call upon the name of Jesus shall be saved.*"

This last verse I've shared does not say that if you call upon the name of Jesus you *might be* saved, it says you *shall be saved!* What an important statement this is! The word *shall* means that you are 100 percent saved and sealed until the day that Jesus comes.

Life is not over yet for you, my friend. You still have time to be saved if you need to be saved. You can still make a positive impact on the world around you! God is not through with you, and He still wants to use you to win others and to rescue them from slipping off the edge and falling into the pits of hell. Who are you going to listen to? How are you going to respond? Will you allow Satan to silence you, or will you accept whatever it is that God is giving you and move on for the cause of Christ? I want to challenge you today to make prayer a daily part of your life! Exercise your faith like you've never done so before! Claim the promises that God has in store for you! Last, but not least, love and live like you've never loved and lived before, remembering that God wants absolutely the very best there is for you! May the blessing and peace of God fill your hearts and minds today and forevermore!

> Revelation 22:12–14—"And behold, I come quickly; and my reward is with me, to give to every man according as his work shall be. I am the Alpha and Omega, the beginning and the end, the first and the last. Blessed are they that do his commandments, that they may have right to the tree of life, and may enter in through the gates into the city."

A Minute of Meditation

As someone who accepted what Christ had to offer me at a very young age, I really feel like I avoided a lot of major detours that I may have taken otherwise. I will be the first to tell you, though, that once you accept Christ, that Satan will work a lot harder on you than he does when you are living a life of sin. Your acceptance of Christ simply means you have taken a stand, and you are saying you believe. You have asked for forgiveness, God has forgiven you, and Satan has lost control of you and your eternal destiny from that moment on. However, my friends, Satan will not let up! As a matter of fact, you will begin to notice that he is going to be after you now more than ever before. Why? Because he wants to *silence* you! Satan wants to rob you of your joy and will take drastic measures to attempt this! He wants you to believe his lies and will work overtime on your thoughts, your attitude, and your actions, and he will use your greatest weaknesses as a tool to try to drag you right back out into the sea of sin. I would ask you to memorize the following verse and quote it to Satan every time he tries to bring you down. It's a great promise straight from the heart of God and a wonderful reminder that your sins have been cast into the sea of forgetfulness, never to be remembered ever again! Blessings today and always!

> *"And I give unto them eternal; and they shall NEVER perish, neither shall any man pluck them out of my hand."*

Printed in the USA
CPSIA information can be obtained
at www.ICGtesting.com
LVHW072301300723
753806LV00015B/224